THE LORD'S
PATTERN FOR
PRAYER

PETER MASTERS

THE WAKEMAN TRUST * LONDON

THE LORD'S PATTERN FOR PRAYER

© Peter Masters 2003

THE WAKEMAN TRUST
(UK Registered Charity)
Website: www.wakemantrust.org
UK Registered Office
38 Walcot Square
London SE11 4TZ
US Office
300 Artino Drive
Oberlin, OH 44074-1263

ISBN 1 870855 36 1

Cover design by Andrew Owen

Printed by Stephens & George, Merthyr Tydfil, UK

THE LORD'S
PATTERN FOR
PRAYER

CONTENTS

1

A Lesson From Christ

'After this manner therefore pray ye . . .'

Proof for a Pattern Prayer

'The ruins of my soul repair,
And make my heart a house of prayer.'
Charles Wesley

WE MAY TRACE the term 'The Lord's Prayer' back to Cyprian (of Carthage), about AD 250, although its use as a recited prayer probably precedes even that date. In our day it is a very moving fact that millions of unreached, unconverted people know this much about the true faith – they know how to say the Lord's Prayer. What right do we have to delve into and amplify the lines of this most famous of all prayers? Should it not be regarded as 'sacrosanct' and kept as a recited prayer?

We must explore it, because it was primarily intended by the Lord to be a *pattern*, or style, or scheme, or outline of prayer topics and encouragements which would inspire and shape our prayers. It is supremely an agenda for prayer. John Calvin said long ago that its importance lay not so much in the literal words as in their content, which should be expounded. Here, very briefly, are three indications that the Lord's Prayer is chiefly meant as a lesson and an outline:

1 In this book we shall study the Lord's Prayer as given in *Matthew 6.9-13*, but in *Luke's Gospel* the Lord's Prayer follows the request of the disciples, 'Lord, teach us to pray.' The most natural understanding of this request is that they wanted more than a set form of words. They did not primarily ask – 'teach us a prayer' – but – 'teach us how to pray.'

2 When the Lord taught the same prayer on that other occasion (recorded in *Luke 11.1-4*) He put it slightly differently, with five modest variations including one entirely different word, and with the doxology omitted. If He had intended to teach a strict form of prayer for reciting only, He would perhaps have given precisely the same prayer on both occasions.

3 It is also extremely significant that all the petitions are very short, suggesting that they were intended to serve as headings. For example, 'Forgive us our debts' provides only four words of repentance, when we know from other prayers in the Bible that appeals for forgiveness should be more lengthy than that. When the believer repents, he must be conscious of his sins, or at least, of his worst sins, ashamed of them, and ready to name and turn from them. An unspecific, four-word repentance is not enough.

Similarly, all the other petitions have a greater significance than the obvious meaning, such as the opening words of the Lord's Prayer – 'Our Father' – which are designed to draw the soul near to God by reminding us of His great fatherliness and kindness. Similarly, the next phrase – 'which art in heaven' – is more than a description of God's location, but reminds us of His infinite majesty and power. Tertullian, writing in the second century, said this prayer was as 'copious in meaning as it is condensed in expression'. Each petition has a grand objective. There are no vague or merely poetic petitions, nor any repetition or overlapping thoughts. Here is a full range of topics to be included in our prayers, but in our personal praying we are meant to go into greater detail.

For How Long Should We Pray?

If the writer may inject a personal comment – at the beginning of the Christian life I found one aspect of prayer extremely intimidating, because I had gained the impression that for prayer to be worthwhile, you had to be on your knees for hours. Heroes of prayer (such as the famous 'Praying Hyde') were frequently held up in messages and books as the people to be imitated, although few seemed able to come near to their achievements. Looking back, I think it would have been very helpful for someone to have advised a prayer time of fifteen minutes a day (Bible reading extra) as a minimum standard – especially for a beginner – with extra prayer being made as opportunity or necessity arose. It is important to mention this as the contents of this book will suggest many lines of prayer that could not possibly be all used together.

To spend longer in prayer is unquestionably right and precious, and every Christian should strive for this, but a basic, regular, readily achievable standard will deliver many from the opposite extreme, namely, a few stumbled sentences a day. Although we have argued that the Lord's Prayer is ideally seen as an outline or a set of headings, it is nevertheless rather compact in design, and other prayers in the Bible are never unduly long. We learn from this that prayer does not always have to strive for length. On the other hand, our Saviour and perfect example is reported to have prayed all night, and so we too must at times pray at length. Nevertheless, a basic standard will keep us under the smile of God, close to Him, and experiencing His power and blessing in our lives.

Whether we are currently praying for fifteen minutes each day or for longer, the content of our prayers, and the different 'kinds' of petition that we make, will always be best ordered and most enriched by keeping in view the pattern prayer of the Lord, in Whose name we pray.

2

The Way to Address God

'Our Father'

Preparing the Heart for Prayer

'O Thou, by Whom we come to God,
The Life, the Truth, the Way,
The path of prayer Thyself hast trod:
Lord, teach us how to pray!'
James Montgomery

WE OFTEN find it difficult to pray because our hearts are cold and unfeeling. How can we be helped to come into the presence of God with the depth of desire and warmth of heart that we long to have? The best answer is here at the beginning of the Lord's Prayer – 'Our Father'. The very term 'Father' should help us draw near, for many thoughts are compressed into this word. It is right, of course, to regard God as an almighty being or a king, but to believers He is also a Father, revealing His amazing fatherliness, affection and care for His people.

In one sense He is Father of all, through creation, and all will answer to Him. All are obligated to honour, serve, and obey Him, for as Father, He looks upon all, even though the outcome of His watching will be to bring many into judgement. However, He is Father in a special and intimate way to all who have experienced the new birth and been adopted into the divine family. To say 'Our Father' in prayer, is to derive assurance along the following lines.

1. The Father's Approachability

First, the term 'Father' suggests *resemblance and approachability*. We say this with care and reverence, because He is holy and infinite in all His attributes, and obviously we are not. There is not a great resemblance, but there is a significant resemblance, and this helps us to approach Him. We do not think of our earthly fathers as strange beings from another planet, because we resemble them; they are related and similar, and so it is with the Almighty Father. We do not worship a being Who is entirely beyond our comprehension for, like Him, we are personal beings. Like Him we have the power of reason, except that His is infinite and glorious. Like Him we have the power of speech or communication. He deigns to give Himself the name of Father partly to remind us of these resemblances, and this is highly encouraging to us.

Because we are made in His image, we can grasp that He is a listening God with a Father's heart. By adopting the title *Father*, God extends to us an invitation and a right to pray, saying, in effect, 'You are My children and I am approachable, and will hear and deal with you.' It is said that the culture of Bible times did not allow a servant to call his master 'father', but only the children could do this. Seen in this light, Almighty God's use of the term 'Father' takes on special meaning. 'You may call Me Father,' He says, 'not being slaves or servants, but children, and I will receive you.'

2. The Father's Paternal Kindness

Secondly, the word 'Father' tells us that *paternal kindness is to be expected* from Him. When your earthly father says something especially nice to you or gives you something, whether you are a child or an adult, you do not say, 'What an astonishing thing that I, a complete nobody, should have been shown this kindness.' As a child you do not find it amazing that your father should work to keep a roof over your head and food on the table. None of these things strikes you as strange, because he is your father, and paternal care and kindness is to be expected. No young child returns home after school wondering whether his father will recognise him, or speak to him. With the Lord, also, paternal kindness is *assured*, and this is a powerful encouragement to the people of God. When we pray, we need never be anxious, fearing that God will turn toward us a hard and unyielding face, for our God styles Himself as Father.

Children err and disobey constantly but a father cannot hold it against them perpetually. He must forgive, otherwise home would be a nightmare. How much kinder is Almighty God in Whom are all the paternal attributes to an infinite degree. He enjoys His children, pities and sympathises with them, inclines His heart toward them, and He bestows gifts and blessings regardless of their inadequacies. A father does not sell things to his children, but gives them freely, and similarly the Lord withholds nothing which is right and proper. In naming Himself as our Father the Lord has pledged His fatherly love to us.

3. The Father's Right to our Trust

Thirdly, the term 'Father' tells us that *the Lord has a right to our faith* in prayer. This is particularly well illustrated with younger children who always respect their father, except, perhaps, when he has to punish them. Children look up to their father, generally never doubting that whatever he undertakes, he is able to do. If the father drives the family on holiday, a child does not sit in the back of the car thinking, 'Can my father possibly do this? I didn't know he could drive a car so far. I never imagined he could get us safely to the destination.' Such doubt is not in the nature of a child, who naturally considers that his earthly father is big, and can cope with all these things. How offensive it is to God if believers doubt that He can deal with their situation. The term 'Father' is a reminder that we must approach God with respect, and trust Him entirely.

4. The Father's Knowledge of His Children

Fourthly, the term 'Father' identifies One Who knows all about us, and therefore *openness and repentance are essential* to our approach. A father knows what his children are like, for he reads their personalities and observes their misdemeanours. Even as we say, 'Our Father', we should be filled with a realisation that the divine Father knows our every thought and motive, and scans in a moment our entire life history. He saw us at birth, and at our new birth. He knows what we have promised Him, and how much we owe to Him. This thought would be terrifying if it were not for the fact that He is a Father Who would never destroy His children. Our daily faults are open to His view, and therefore as we approach Him, repentance is called for.

5. The Father's Standards

Fifthly, the term 'Father' demands that *we conform to His rules and standards*. This corrects a great mistake in prayer, for believers are inclined to pray for many provisions and blessings without making sure that they are actively complying with God's rules and laws.

They may have turned aside from striving to obey Him in the development of personal character, and from pleasing Him by word and deed. A father cannot be expected to give privileges and benefits to children who defy and displease him. If I have lost my conscientious desire to please Him, and yet I pray, 'Oh, my heavenly Father', I cannot truly mean those words. If we have no serious intention of controlling and subduing sin and promoting holiness, we should not expect our prayers to be answered. Our Father's household has ten prime commandments branching into many jewels of conduct and character, including the famous 'fruit of the Spirit' of *Galatians 5*. It also has rules for Christian service which must be respected, honoured and aimed for, and the very title 'Father' reminds us of such standards – the rules of the heavenly household.

> Implicit in all these issues is our duty of gratitude. As we reflect on each one, we praise and thank the Source and Provider of all our spiritual and temporal blessings.

6. The Father's Other Children

Sixthly, the term 'Father' (particularly *our* Father) stirs our responsibility to *other members of the family*. In this family we are not the only child. To pray in a manner which is acceptable to God we must present ourselves as members of His family, humbly recognising fellow believers, preserving fraternal harmony, and serving the Father in the family 'team'. An aloof person, who detaches himself from the fellowship of God's people, adopting an independent, critical spirit, cannot truly pray, 'Our Father'. An indifferent, uncaring or lazy person, who is not touched by the needs and trials of brothers and sisters, and who gives no help to them in their work for the Lord, cannot say, 'Our Father' except in a hypocritical way. God's chosen appellation brings conviction and direction.

7. The Father's Provision and Guidance

Seventhly, the term 'Father' naturally identifies the Lord as One Who will *guide and protect* His people. The ideal father directs and shapes the life of his child. He steers his offspring through childhood and youth, and provides for him. It follows that when we approach God in prayer, we must have an appreciation of His *providence*. Sometimes believers rush into the presence of God asking for help with problems, and for all manner of benefits, the emphasis of their prayer being – 'Help me; deliver me; give me!' At times it must sound to God as if we are saying – though we would not dare – 'Oh, Lord, You abandon me to innumerable difficulties so that I have to cry out for help. You don't seem to know what is happening to me, or care about the trials that I have; You don't have Your hand upon me; nevertheless, I am glad that You are there for emergencies.'

This, of course, is insulting to Him. When we pray the word, 'Father', we should think to ourselves, 'Because He is a perfect Father everything is under His control. He always knows what He is doing. I believe in the providence of God, and therefore if some calamity has happened in my life, I will not pray as a desperate victim. I will go to Him in the certainty that He knows what has happened, has allowed it, and will bring good out of it. I will ask Him for blessing and strength, not in a hopeless, distracted, aggrieved way, but in a trusting way. This trial will help me to pray and to exercise faith. Certainly it will be for my eternal, spiritual good, for all things are in His hands, I am His child, and He will never let me out of His fatherly oversight.' The term 'Father' means all that.

8. The Father's House Our Home

Eighthly, the term 'Father' speaks of the One Whose 'home' we share and to which we have access. We may enter the house at any time and walk around as though we owned the place – as children do. The term 'Father' includes the privilege of *belonging*. It is quite difficult to teach a small child to respect particular rooms in the house, because to that child it is not just the parents' house, it is *his* house also. Believers know instinctively that they may live before God in His spiritual house, His church, as those who belong there. This is *our* place. We may put our feet under the table as those who have a filial right. We may enjoy the furnishings, fittings and fixtures, and admire the distinctive views from its windows. We may freely enjoy the household of faith, with all its glories. Here we drink from the wells of the Word of God, experience the blessings, and observe closely the words and actions of our God, and one day, when faith yields to sight, we shall enjoy these glories in all their fulness for all eternity.

To be in the family of God means that we may relish Christian experience, hear His voice, and rejoice before Him, as insiders. We may draw near to Him, always with reverence, but also in a familiar manner, as children, crying, 'Abba, Father!' If sometimes wayward and backslidden, feeling alienated and removed, we nevertheless know the way home, and will go in repentance and desire through the porch of prayer and into the throne room within, to call upon 'Our Father'. The term 'Father' is about freedom of access.

9. The Father's Enduring Fatherhood

Ninthly, the term 'Father' teaches us almost as no other word in the Bible about our *eternal security*. We may backslide or grow cold, but He will at length draw us back, by chastisement if necessary, and we shall never be lost. After all, you can never cease to be your father's child. People speak about their ex-wife or ex-husband, but no one talks about an ex-child. If you should move away, even to the furthest end of the earth, you remain your father's child. Even after death, should you predecease him, you will remain his child, and he will think of you as such. That God should call Himself the Father of believers is the most concrete token of eternal security, and it tells us we are His children for ever.

The security breathed by the term 'Father' was never more wonderfully expressed than in the old London Confession of Faith of Baptists in 1689, where we are given these dramatic words:

'And though many storms and floods arise and beat against them *[believers]*, yet these shall never be able to take them off that foundation and rock which by faith they are fastened upon; notwithstanding through unbelief and the temptations of Satan, the sensible sight of the light and love of God may for a time be clouded and obscured, yet He is still the same, and they shall be sure to be kept by the power of God unto salvation, where they shall enjoy their purchased possession; they being engraven upon the palms of His hands, and their names having been written in the Book of Life from all eternity.'

The Fulness of Fatherliness

If only we could remember all that is implied in the term 'Father', we would draw near to the Lord with greater gratitude, love and assurance. It tells us that He is personal and relational, and we may therefore draw near. It tells us we may count on His paternal kindness. It tells us that we must approach Him with respectful faith, trusting that He is mighty. It tells us that He sees us, and that we must be open before Him and repent of sin. It tells us that we must earnestly try to conform to His standards in order to be heard by Him. It tells us we must live in harmony with our spiritual family in order to please Him. It tells us to respect His wise providence and His management of our lives. It tells us of our special position in His household, and it assures us of our eternal security. Implicit in all these issues is our duty of gratitude. As we reflect on each one, we praise and thank the Source and Provider of all our spiritual and temporal blessings. The opening words of the Lord's Prayer say so much, so that even before our petitions begin, we are blessed.

3

The Way to Address God

'Which art in heaven'

How Great is Your God?

'Now let our souls on wings sublime
Rise from the vanities of time,
Draw back the parting veil, and see
The glories of eternity.'
Thomas Gibbons

EVERY PHRASE of this magnificent pattern prayer is full of guidance, and this one supplies in just four words a great lesson about the adoration of God. We lose much if we read over these words too swiftly because they are more than a mere identification of the Father's whereabouts. It is a phrase calculated to build within us a worthy attitude or approach to the Lord. When the heart is cold, and spiritual feelings are running dry, these simple words, rightly understood, will lift the believer up to a renewed appreciation of God's glory, and to great sincerity and fervour. At least six magnificent thoughts are implied here to shape our attitude as we pray, leading us into a true engagement with the Lord.

1. The Father's Immensity and Power

First, the phrase – 'which art in heaven' – reminds us of the *greatness of God*. Of course, He is everywhere, but He is to be particularly addressed as the One Who inhabits the Heaven of heavens, because this will stir within us a sense of spiritual realism and perspective. It will cause us to think on a large scale, as we ought to. Heaven is the dwelling-place of the transcendent God, the great Creator, to Whom the entire universe is an immeasurably tiny speck. To address God in these terms reminds us of His supremacy and His unimaginable immensity and power, raising our thoughts, and stimulating our reverence. Pride melts away before such a God, and we are suffused with a deep sense of privilege. Impressed upon us is our smallness, and the Lord's greatness. He becomes to us our mighty and glorious Lord – 'the Great, the Holy, and the High'.

Today, tragically, superficiality and informality abound in much prayer and worship. Showmanship and entertainment dominate. Believers often stride into God's presence in prayer lacking all sense of occasion, and with a small awareness of His sublime dignity as King of kings and Lord of lords.

The phrase – 'which art in heaven' – makes us feel like the grasshoppers of *Isaiah 40*, or as mere specks of dust before Him, so that we appreciate all the more the fact that He looks upon us fondly, as children. With this view of the Lord, our style of prayer is also lifted up, for how can we present before such a Father a catalogue of minor, subjective, temporal requests? We feel compelled to focus first on great and spiritual needs for the glory of His name. 'Which art in heaven' therefore melts our hearts, calls us to reverence, and brings to life for us the perspective expressed by the hymnwriter –

There, there on eagle-wing we soar,
And time and sense seem all no more:
And Heaven comes down our souls to greet,
And glory crowns the mercy-seat.

2. The Father's Spiritual Being

Secondly, the phrase – 'which art in heaven' – impresses upon the mind that God *is a heavenly God* and a *spirit*, not an *earthly* being. He is not, like us, a weak and fallible mortal. Certainly, we are made in His image in a number of respects, but He is of another essence, and vastly beyond us. He cannot be physically seen or touched. He is the mysterious, incomprehensible, invisible God, the one and only self-existent Spirit-being, the unfathomable Three-in-One. This thought reinforces our realisation that prayer may only be communicated to such a God *by faith*. To sense or feel Him in a definite, physical, concrete way would merely be an exercise of imagination, emotionalism or mysticism. There is undoubtedly an emotional aspect to prayer, because the realisation that we are received by God, and may be blessed by Him, is immensely moving. Also, the Lord graciously assures our hearts and comforts us as we pray, but this is not the same as 'feeling' God. Nor should we work up a sense of God for ourselves, or make it our primary goal. We pray *by faith*, which means that we come before God believing that our thoughts will be winged all the way to God's glorious throne by the power of the Holy Spirit, through the reconciling work of Christ. Because we are creatures of the earth, the only way to be heard in Heaven is to speak by faith in Christ, trusting entirely that through Him we may be heard. And if at times our emotions will not co-operate to give us joy and peace as we pray, it makes no difference, because what really matters is faith, and that is essentially an exercise of the mind. Emotions are a kind gift of God and a great blessing, but we can if necessary pray without them (as the psalmist does in *Psalm 42*). Simple faith is everything!

3. The Father's Sovereignty and Timelessness

Thirdly, to acknowledge that the Father is in Heaven is to remember that *He is outside time*. He has enclosed this universe in an envelope of time, but He is the Creator of time, and Lord over it, reigning from His eternal dwelling-place in Heaven. We must therefore approach Him as the One Who superintends all events, Who views the entire history of the universe, as well as the history of our individual lives in their minutest detail, all the time.

While on earth we are intimidated by time. We are harassed and worried by it, often being afraid of what will happen next, or of when and how events will take place. But to address God as being in Heaven reassures us that He knows all that is going on, and that His scheme for us will be perfectly worked out. In times of trouble we realise that God has the outcome in hand. He knows what He is training us or chastising us for. He is above time, and has a sovereign plan. No event in time can thwart the purpose of the timeless, infallible God, Who determines our lifespan.

The phrase – 'which art in heaven' – therefore draws attention to God as Landlord of a universe which He has set in the dimension of time. It helps us to come with trust and contentment when we address the One Who operates from a lofty throne.

4. The Father's Amazing Condescension

Fourthly, the fact that God is in Heaven stirs us to appreciate *the extent of His condescension*. He is high and lifted up – the Supreme Being dwelling in eternal glory and bliss. What has He to do with earth? Why should He look upon puny, objectionable rebels who have brought themselves under the curse of a fallen, sin-sick world? Is our world not utterly offensive to Him? Yet the almighty, holy Father in Heaven stoops down to show undeserved kindness to a sinful, distasteful people. He considers us, and His great heart of love beats for us. The One Who has the angelic host worshipping Him in purity and perfection, reaches far, far down to sinful worms, even sending the second Person of the Trinity to come to suffer in appalling agony, and die for us.

By incomparable condescension the eternal Father listens to our whispered prayers so tainted by unbelief and selfishness. When we pray – 'which art in heaven' – we should be reminded of the extent to which God has stooped down to relate to us. It should always seem amazing to us that Scripture can say – 'Eye hath not seen, nor ear heard, neither have entered into the heart of man, the things which God hath prepared for them that love him.'

5. The Father's Perfection and Purity

Fifthly, the phrase – 'which art in heaven' – communicates the *holiness of God.* He is seen as being from somewhere other than this sinful realm, and very far from it. He is in Heaven, a pure and perfect domain, far beyond all corruption. In the Lord's Prayer we honour Him for this. This realisation reminds us again that in order to approach Him we must first pause to search our hearts and sincerely repent of all our sin, because He is enthroned in the place of sublime purity. If we did this *every* time we prayed, we would be much more concerned about dealing with our sins. If there is no concern for holiness, and no longing to advance in character, how can the believer expect a meaningful audience with the Holy God? A person of inconsistent life and aim should not expect to receive anything from the Lord, as James warns, saying, 'Let not that man think that he shall receive any thing of the Lord.' We are taught to say, in effect, 'Our Father, which art in the holy Heaven, clothed in a blaze of purity and perfection . . . ' How can we approach Him lightly or hypocritically?

6. The Father's Seat of Blessing

Finally, to address the Father as being in Heaven impresses upon us the stark contrast between Heaven and earth, and the hopelessness of looking to this world for real help, happiness, and lasting blessing. We must direct our prayers from earth to Heaven; from the fallible to the infallible; from the realm of the dying to the realm of the eternal. In this phrase, 'which art in heaven', we are trained to consciously look up to the God Who is the exclusive source of help and satisfaction, and to expect little from this world. We must put no great trust in its notable names or its swelling promises. The only truly mighty and lasting achievement wrought in this world was the life and work of the eternal Son, Who came from Heaven, and has now returned to Heaven. So we must address the Father as being in Heaven, realising that in so doing we make a double statement – that this world cannot satisfy, and that our greatest hopes and needs can only be met from Heaven. With this understanding we will be less shocked and disappointed at this world's failings, and less drawn by covetous desires.

'Which art in heaven' may appear to be a simple phrase, but it brings thoughts to the mind which shape our approach in prayer. It humbles the believer with a realisation of the immensity of the Lord, laying a foundation of awe and reverence. It tells us that God is not *earthly* but *spiritual.* Therefore He must be approached by faith. It places Him outside time and the created order, pointing to His superintendence and providence, and stirring our trust and confidence. It opens our eyes to the condescension of God, Who stoops so far to show lovingkindness to His people. By this means it moves us to value our privileges, and to love and adore Him. It puts up a hand to warn us of the purity of God, and the need for cleansing and holiness as we approach Him. It reinforces our awareness that we are not of this world, which has nothing for us, but we look to the Lord alone for the great needs of life.

4

The First Petition
'Hallowed be thy name'

How Shall I Praise the Eternal God?

'Our heavenly Father, hear
The prayer we offer now;
Thy name be hallowed far and near,
To Thee shall all flesh bow.'
James Montgomery

TO HALLOW means to honour as holy, and to hallow the name of God means to recognise that name as glorious, sacred and perfect. Why hallow the *name* of God? The *name* of God in Scripture represents His divine being and attributes. To hallow God's name, therefore, is to acknowledge and thoughtfully appreciate His attributes or characteristics. We admire them as *infinitely* marvellous. We say from our hearts that they are free from the slightest taint of impurity, and also wonderful in the way they harmonise together. In God there is no discord, no contradiction, and no inconsistency.

To hallow God's name is an act of praise, but it is also a prayer, in which we ask that the attributes of God may be grasped and valued with awe and wonder by many more people. It is very significant that in this pattern prayer the Saviour made this the very first petition. Before we consider which attributes we are to mention, it will be helpful to see how highly effective this first petition is in checking three dangerous influences that would ruin reverence and respect in prayer.

1. A Brake on Presumption

Because of human weakness, prayer carries a potentially dangerous side effect. It is, after all, an amazing privilege of intimacy, and this familiarity may certainly reduce our reverence for God. To aggravate this possibility, our access to Him is so *easy*. We may approach Him at any time, anywhere, and be assured of an immediate reception. He is available without appointment, and we may consume as much of His attention as we like. These very blessings can lead to a failure to revere His might and majesty. Everyone knows that human beings tend not to respect people (or things) who can be *easily* approached. In the Old Testament system of worship people were trained by awe-inspiring proceedings including symbols and rituals which had the effect of isolating God from a casual approach. The symbolism certainly said that God was among them, but it also said that He was a holy God Who must be approached with fear and trembling.

In Christ, this sense of distance is removed, along with the fear and trembling. We may come running into the presence of the Lord, and this may lead to a loss of respect for Him. Christian people find it is easier to have an audience with God than with the managing director of their firm. In many ways the latter may seem to be of greater significance or importance. To begin prayer by recognising the holiness of God's infinite attributes, is an essential antidote to this presumptuous spirit.

2. A Check on Spoiling

The need for such a petition also arises because we approach God the Father in the merit of Christ the Son. He has paid for us to come, not we ourselves. Christ having offered up His perfect righteousness for us, salvation and access to God is not only easy, it is *free*, and, sadly, this too may cause a loss of appreciation. The Lord is easily sought and freely found.

When churches support the distribution of Christian literature in needy parts of the world they are often told by local pastors, 'Don't make it entirely free, because if you do it will not be taken seriously, or valued.' Likewise, free access to God may diminish our esteem for both the blessing and the Giver. To make matters still worse, we are able to ask God for small as well as large things. In His condescending love, the Lord of glory makes Himself as available as the old-fashioned corner shop, providing the very smallest helps. This, too, because we are foolish, robs us of appreciation of His greatness and His glorious perfections. To spend some time sincerely hallowing the majestic attributes of God will save us from this error.

3. A Check on Disrespect Arising from Ignorance

Our small grasp of the sheer greatness of God also robs us of reverence. We are never awed by the sight of the divine majesty, because God is invisible to us. If He were to give us just a little glimpse of His mighty being, we would be terrified. He does not, however, overawe us by an audible voice, powerful as many waters, and nothing daunting is put in the way of our approach to Him. We are invited to come in a familiar way. Even when we sin, God does not thunder from the skies, rebuking us for our failings. In fallen human beings, fear promotes respect, yet we have no cause to be afraid of Him. The remedy of Christ for our tendency to lose reverence and appreciation is not to take away our peace, or to show us a more severe face, but to teach us to pray, 'Hallowed be thy name.' He trains us to maintain reverence and humility by considering and acknowledging the attributes of God at the beginning of our prayers. Surely, we must name at least some of these attributes, and admire them, but how can we do this if we have never committed them to memory?

It has been said that 'Hallowed be thy name' sounds like a prayer *for* God, as though God needs us to pray for Him. This, of course, is not the case. First, this petition is intended to be a clear recognition of God's attributes. Secondly, it is a statement of submission to God. Thirdly, it is a prayer that God's perfections will be worshipped and adored by many more people. Fourthly, it is an affirmation that God will one day disclose His glory to all – even to the rebellious as they go to judgement.

How to Exalt God's Attributes

How should I praise God's attributes? Obviously, I must speak of the sole, self-existent Creator Who alone possesses life, and I must articulate that. I must say, 'Lord, Thou art the only eternal being, and everything that exists comes from Thee.' For an inspired example of hallowing the characteristics of God we may turn to *Jeremiah 10.6-7, 10* and *12*. Here is a perfect example.

'Forasmuch as there is none like unto thee, O Lord; thou art great, and thy name is great in might. Who would not fear thee, O King of nations? for to thee doth it appertain: forasmuch as among all the wise men of the nations, and in all their kingdoms, there is none like unto thee . . .

'But the Lord is the true God, he is the living God, and an everlasting king: at his wrath the earth shall tremble, and the nations shall not be able to abide his indignation . . . He hath made the earth by his power, he hath established the world by his wisdom, and hath stretched out the heavens by his discretion.'

Psalm 71 makes particular mention of the holiness and perfection of God in the fifteenth verse, where the psalmist says: 'My mouth shall shew forth thy righteousness and thy salvation all the day; for I know not the numbers thereof.'

Numerous great worship hymns begin with this recognition of the eternal, infinite being of God, and of His might and majesty. Consider these examples from Isaac Watts, who wrote many hymns beginning in the manner taught in the Lord's Prayer. (In these verses the references to God's attributes are highlighted in capital letters.)

> *How shall I praise the ETERNAL God,*
> *That INFINITE Unknown?*
> *Who can ascend His high abode,*
> *Or venture near His throne?*
>
> *The great INVISIBLE! He dwells*
> *Concealed in dazzling light;* *[HOLINESS]*
> *But His all-searching eye reveals*
> *The secrets of the night.* *[KNOWLEDGE]*
>
> *Those watchful eyes, that never sleep,*
> *Survey the world around;*
> *His WISDOM is a boundless deep,*
> *Whose depths we cannot sound.*
>
> *He knows NO SHADOW OF A CHANGE,*
> *Nor alters His decrees;*

> *Firm as a rock His* TRUTH *remains,*
>   *To guard His promises.*

> JUSTICE *upon an awesome throne*
>   *Maintains the rights of God;*
> *While* MERCY *sends her pardons down,*
>   *Bought with a Saviour's blood.*

In the case of this hymn, it is not until the last verse that the worshipper considers his own needs:

> *Now to my soul,* IMMORTAL KING,
>   *Speak Thy forgiving word,*
> *That it may be my joy to sing*
>   *The mercies of my* LORD.

Another hymn of Watts begins with the same lofty, objective approach that focuses on the greatness of God:

> *Eternal Power! Whose high abode*
> *Befits the grandeur of our God –*
> *Unending space beyond the bounds*
> *Where stars revolve their little rounds.*

> *Thee while the first archangel sings,*
> *He hides his face beneath his wings,*
> *And throngs of shining ones around,*
> *Fall worshipping upon the ground.*

> *Lord, what shall earth and ashes do?*
> *We would adore our Maker too;*
> *From sin and dust to Thee we cry,*
> *The Great, the Holy, and the High!*

Yet another verse so typical of Watts is . . .

> *Begin my tongue a heavenly theme,*
>   *Of boundless wonders sing:*
> *The mighty works and holy name*
>   *Of our eternal King!*

Hymnwriters of the past certainly understood what the Saviour meant when He commanded us to pray – 'Hallowed be thy name.' We must mention the attributes of Almighty God, and praise and adore Him for them, not only as pastors leading public prayer, but also in personal prayer. Objective praise comes before subjective needs in the pattern prayer. We may certainly pray – 'We thank Thee, Lord, that the earth is so beautiful,' but not ideally at the very beginning of our prayer. First, we should remember *Who* God is, and give glory to Him, acknowledging Him as the God of providence Who knows and plans and sees, so that all that happens to us happens by His permission. We are to acknowledge *His* power and might and lordship in all areas of life, thoughtfully appreciating Him as we do so. Let us not rush into requests without first thinking, 'Who is my God? Who is the One to Whom I pray?'

God's Lesson to Moses

To put the attributes of God first in prayer is a practice taught in many scriptures aside from the Lord's Prayer. *Exodus 34.5-7* has a wonderful lesson in prayer:

'And the Lord descended in the cloud, and stood with him *[Moses]* there, and proclaimed the name of the Lord. And the Lord passed by before him, and proclaimed, The Lord, the Lord God, merciful and gracious, longsuffering, and abundant in goodness and truth, keeping mercy for thousands, forgiving iniquity and transgression and sin, and that will by no means clear the guilty.'

'Hallowed be thy name' means that we echo these God-given sentiments. The Lord in speaking to Moses makes mention of His mercy, together with His grace, goodness, truth and justice. All are there.

The supreme exhibition of how the holy attributes of God work in perfect harmony is seen on the cross of Calvary, as we remind ourselves often. We see there the justice and the righteousness of God. He must punish sin, and be faithful to His justice. Yet He desires also to give expression to His great mercy, kindness, grace and goodness in providing salvation. When Christ suffered the penalty of human sin, justice joined with mercy to demonstrate the harmony of God's attributes. 'Hallowed be thy name' is another way of praying that God's attributes displayed on Calvary may be grasped and loved by countless human minds.

Those Who Cannot Hallow God's Name

Ministers, scholars known as theological liberals, and all other people who do not believe in the inspired, infallible Scripture and the divinity and lordship of Christ cannot honestly pray, 'Hallowed be thy name,' because they do not believe that the eternal Son was infallible. They do not accept the truthfulness of His record, or that He was right in His interpretation of the Old Testament. They believe He made mistakes, and was unable to forecast where all His activities would lead Him. By their blasphemous ideas they really say, 'Lord, may Thy name and attributes not be hallowed. May they be seen as merely human and full of imperfections.'

Alarmingly, even sincere Bible-believing Christians may be disqualified in God's sight from saying, 'Hallowed be thy name.' This disqualification is published in *Jeremiah 9.23-24*:

'Thus saith the Lord, Let not the wise man glory in his wisdom, neither let the mighty man glory in his might, let not the rich man glory in his riches: but let him that glorieth glory in this, that he understandeth and knoweth me, that I am the Lord which exercise lovingkindness, judgment, and righteousness, in the earth: for in these things I delight, saith the Lord.'

The challenge here is – How can we pray, 'Hallowed be thy name,' if our hearts are dominated by pride, self-confidence and self-reliance? Such pride eclipses true and total reverence for God, because we cannot say, 'Lord, I depend on Thee for everything. Even my natural abilities are of no use if Thou art not with me. If Thy blessing is not upon my work, my relationships, and my spiritual service, I cannot be pleasing before Thee.' Only after having cleared away proud self-confidence may we truly appreciate the attributes of God.

May the being and attributes of God be hallowed and appreciated in my praise! May I act in a way that is consistent with this petition! Even as I pray that God's name will be appreciated in the world, may my personal testimony contribute to that end. May I support and encourage God's messengers, strengthening them to proclaim His qualities to vast numbers of people! When I next pray, before proceeding into detailed petitions, may I worthily hallow the name of God, in my own words, and at greater length than the abridged lesson given in the pattern prayer. May His perfections be lifted up and acknowledged, and great glory brought to His holy name!

5

The Second Petition

'Thy kingdom come'

Seeing the Difference Between Earth and Heaven

'Dark, dark has been the midnight,
But dayspring is at hand,
And glory, glory dwelleth
In Emmanuel's land.'
Anne Ross Cousin

THE SECOND petition in our Lord's perfect pattern prayer is, 'Thy kingdom come.' We must be aware of the difference between the second and third petitions. The latter reads, 'Thy will be done in earth, as it is in heaven.' Both petitions are about the rule of Almighty God, the difference being that 'Thy kingdom come' concerns the final and eternal goal, whereas 'Thy will be done' is about *how* God will save and prepare people for that goal even now.

'Thy kingdom come' stands back and glories in the fact that God's kingdom is certainly coming, identifies with His plan, and considers how vastly superior it will be to anything in this world. To pray this sincerely requires a clear view of what the heavenly kingdom is like – such as its composition, occupants, blessedness and wonders. 'Thy kingdom come' is chiefly a prayer of humble approval and complete acceptance of whatever God will bring about. We say, in effect, 'Lord, as Thy child, I love with all my heart Thy great and eternal purpose, and I can see the glory of it. Lord, may this glorious kingdom come, in which all sin and pain will be abolished, and perfection and glory will prevail for ever. This kingdom is my highest desire. May the Truth be finally vindicated and the Saviour's purposes fulfilled, and may He reign for all eternity.'

This second petition is quite different from all that has gone before. 'Our Father' – honours Him as Father, and helps us to value, love and trust Him. 'Which art in heaven' – acknowledges His lordship over time and earth, and gives us opportunity to look away from this world and trust Him for everything. 'Hallowed be thy name' – brings us to worship Him, and focus on His attributes. But 'Thy kingdom come' – turns our minds to God's ultimate purpose, and causes us to appreciate with longing the coming kingdom.

The Kingdom Illustration

Almighty God at the present time is rejected and resented by millions of people in this sinful, fallen world, where cruelty and unfairness abound. But the time is coming when this present world will be destroyed, all rebellion crushed, and everything ruined by sin purged, and subsequently restored to perfection. Then God will be vindicated, loved and worshipped eternally. Then there will be no challenge to our victorious Lord, and all the redeemed in Heaven will worship, admire and obey Him for ever.

What will the coming kingdom be like? What avenue of thought and reflection will enable us to pray this petition with sincere desire? The answer lies in the word 'kingdom'. Heaven, as a perfect kingdom, will enshrine all the ideal values and objectives desired by earthly kingdoms, yet never achieved. The 'ideal' for an earthly kingdom provides an illustration of the heavenly.

1 The first feature of God's kingdom is *the King*. In ancient times a land was valued by the greatness of its king. No nation could be considered great if its monarch was weak in defence, or unjust, or lacking in wealth, or indifferent to the hardships of the people. The glory of the kingdom of Heaven is Christ her King, for He is perfect in every respect as ruler. Viewed in terms of greatness and majesty, His power is limitless and His throne is clothed in glory, magnificence, radiance and purity. He is surrounded by millions of angels – an innumerable host of glorious beings – who wait upon Him constantly. No empire or kingdom on earth has ever had a ruler of divine stature, incapable of failure, and overflowing with infinite wisdom and kindness. Christ is in the midst of this kingdom. Here, He is at home with His people.

> *Throughout the universe of bliss,*
> *The centre Thou, and sun;*
> *The eternal theme of praise is this,*
> *To Heaven's belovèd One:*
>
> *Worthy, O Lamb of God, art Thou*
> *That every knee to Thee should bow.*

2 Like earthly kingdoms, the heavenly kingdom has a *defined and guarded border* to keep out intruders and to maintain her blessedness and peace. No defiling thing can enter, nor abomination, nor lie. Outside are 'dogs, and sorcerers, and whoremongers, and murderers, and idolaters, and whosoever loveth and maketh a lie'. This is a place of unfading purity and perfection.

3 The best earthly kingdoms would like to be famed for *benevolence* to the poor and disadvantaged. The heavenly kingdom exceeds them all immeasurably, because her very atmosphere is grace. All who walk there live freely under the smile of the King. There is no painful labour; there are no taxes or dues; there is no purchase price on anything, for Jesus Christ has purchased for His people every benefit to be found there, for ever.

4 Earthly kingdoms require the machinery of *orderly administration*, usually a bureaucracy or civil service. The greater the realm, the larger the apparatus of government, and the greater the remoteness of the people from their ruler. Bureaucracies take time over everything, become condescending, make mistakes and frequently deal unjustly. But the heavenly kingdom has no civil service, only ministering angels who instantly obey the commands of Christ. He, as King, views all His people all the time, and they relate directly with Him. Though vaster and more populous than the greatest earthly empire, God's coming kingdom is a miraculous place of profoundest fellowship with the Lord, and between citizens.

5 Earthly kingdoms are well regarded if there is a measure of *liberty* in them. The perfect government should rule in a way that blends rule and order with liberty, but only in Heaven, the ultimate land of liberty, is this wholly accomplished. In Heaven, all do exactly what they want, because the glorified believer delights to do that which is holy and perfect. All bondage to sinful desires and appetites lies in the past. There is no fear, because fear of loss, of pain, of betrayal, of failure, of disease, or of any other hardship, has gone for ever.

While in this present life, God must keep a disciplining hand on His people to restrain them from sin, but the day is coming when ransomed hearts shall be so perfectly conformed to Him that they shall be given perfect liberty of expression – the citizens of a realm of highest dignity and freedom in which they willingly and gladly delight in God's order.

6 Earthly kingdoms like to claim *equality and fraternity*, but whatever the claims, there are always huge manifestations of inequality and social injustice. Indeed, the economic stability of nations often depends on there being an underclass. There will always be employers and workers, rich and poor, educated and uneducated, privileged and underprivileged, landlords and tenants, and many other distinctions. Every realm is riddled with 'class' and inequity. The sole land of true equality and fraternity is the kingdom of Heaven, where all the King's happy subjects are equal in His sight and enjoy equal provision and blessedness. Here is the place where wealth is entirely shared. Only here is there no rich and poor, no ruling class and underclass, nor contrasting healthy and sick, righteous and wicked, because this is a kingdom of heirs who are equally loved by the King. And here also is the place of perfect fellowship, where there is unrestricted access and harmony between all citizens –

> The sole land of true equality and fraternity is the kingdom of Heaven, where all the King's happy subjects are equal in His sight.

> *And perfect love and friendship reign*
> *Through all eternity.*

7 Earthly kingdoms make laws, and may be judged by the *quality of those laws*. The kingdom of Heaven has the wisest, purest laws, being the commandments of God drawn from His own holy character. As we have noted, nothing contrary to these laws will ever enter, and the people of God will keep them all perfectly, because they have been equipped to do so with sinless hearts. In Heaven God's laws do not serve as a means of curtailing sin by negative commandments and warnings of wrath. In the eternal kingdom

there will be no flesh to mortify or contain, but the 'opposite, positive virtues' of the law will be all-resplendent.

8 Earthly kingdoms may boast *fine buildings, great beauty,* advanced education and high standards of cleanliness, but nothing can be compared with the magnificence of the heavenly realm. When we say, 'Thy kingdom come,' we also look forward to a beauty beyond human comprehension endowed with a unique climate of love, acceptance and enjoyment of God. The eternal realm will have the perfect infrastructure, and the highest imaginable standard of education. Even as we arrive there we shall experience an immense burst of knowledge, and grasp the deep things of God to a degree never imagined on earth. Yet this will only be the beginning, for we shall spend eternity drinking in ever more of the infinite, eternal grandeur and glory of God. Every mind will be emancipated to a condition of intellectual, spiritual brilliance.

It is good to pray for the coming of the kingdom, and we naturally look forward to freedom from all sin, together with perfect happiness and harmony. However, we should not long for these things solely from *our* point of view, but we should desire them for the glory of God, yearning for the time when God will be vindicated and loved by millions of people created and saved by Him. We pray to express our trust that God will make Heaven exactly as He has planned it, to His taste, to be peopled by those He has prepared, and that it will be the zenith of redemption, perfection, happiness and glory.

The Lord Jesus Christ addresses the Father when He teaches us to pray, 'Thy kingdom come,' but we realise that this is also His own kingdom. Certainly it is the kingdom of all the Godhead, but it is particularly spoken of in Scripture as Christ's kingdom because He is the agent of our salvation Who purchased us. He is also the member of the Godhead Who will be our visible King. While on earth, He set Himself as the representative of His people, assuming a lowly position in subordination to the Father, but now that He has ascended up on high and resumed His former glorious station, the kingdom is very particularly *His*.

'Thy kingdom come' is a petition which recognises that these things have not yet been accomplished. This kingdom is still in the future, and what we see in world history is the steady gathering out of souls for salvation. To pray, 'Thy kingdom come,' is not only to identify with God's plan, but also to recognise the extent to which He is progressively building up His eternal realm.

If we understand the Bible correctly, it tells us that towards the end of time there will be a great apostasy and turning away, and surely this is what we now see under way as the end approaches. Soon the day will come when the elements melt with a fervent heat; when God will remake or reconstitute the world in beauty and purity, a magnificent realm beyond our power to imagine. This will be the day for which all creation groans, when we shall have joy unspeakable and full of glory. We must especially desire that great event because *God* will be vindicated and glorified.

Our prayer is, 'Lord, I have tasted Thy kingdom only very slightly in this present life; I long that I may one day see it in all its fulness.' Of course, we cannot pray this prayer sincerely unless we live for the future and not for the present. Do worldly affairs constantly preoccupy and overwhelm us? Do studies, family, or business entirely fill our horizons? Even worse, do we not mind this being so? If we mean this second petition, we shall be moved to live more for that coming kingdom, seeking out the sphere of Christian service that God will assign to us. We may certainly enjoy many things on earth, but should be careful to be balanced. We should say of this world's goods and pleasures – 'So much and no more, lest these become my consuming interest and my gods.' We should be willing to steward and labour against eternity.

Are we doing justice to this essential element of prayer? We must surely pause, align our hearts in identification with God, and say, 'This ultimate goal is the chief thing for me, O Lord. Thy kingdom come.'

6

The Third Petition

'Thy will be done in earth, as it is in heaven'

Affirmation and Submission

'God is a King of power unknown;
Firm are the orders from His throne;
If He resolves – who dare oppose,
Or ask Him why, or what He does?'

Isaac Watts

AS GOD'S WILL is bound to be carried out, how can we pray meaningfully – 'Thy will be done'? Surely this is a pointless petition? Yet this is part of the pattern prayer of the Lord occupying a place high in the order of priorities, being the third out of seven petitions. What, then, is the usefulness of praying for God's will to be carried out? The answer is, this petition (like the first) is more of an *affirmation and submission to God* than a request. It is a statement of total identification with the will of God. There are six leading ways in which we may affirm and desire the will of God, and it is good to pray for each of these in the course of time.

1 Firstly, 'Thy will be done' is an affirmation of the *inevitable victory* of God's will. In saying, 'Thy will be done,' we are in effect saying, 'O, Lord, Thy will is invincible, and will surely come to pass! All Thy plans and promises will be fulfilled!' This petition is an expression of faith in the sovereign will and mighty power of God.

2 Secondly, it is a petition of *appreciation*. We fall before the Lord in total appreciation of the way in which He works, affirming that everything He plans, prescribes, and promises, is faultless and wonderful. 'Thy will be done' is a way of saying, 'Thy will is *perfect.*' We acknowledge that salvation by grace through faith is a marvellous plan, produced by divine genius, and reflecting all the love and the wisdom of God. We bow the knee to the most profound and sublime plan in all the universe. We also admire the intention of the Lord to bring this dispensation of time to an end one day, and to judge the world. We accept without reservation the rightness of the mind and will of God.

3 Thirdly, in this petition we place the emphasis on the word 'Thy' and acknowledge that God's will is not only perfect, but also the *best*, the *essential* and *exclusive* way, as it is, for example, in the work of salvation. There can be no other way, for no other plan could work. Only the atoning death of Christ could deal with sin. Only a work of the Spirit in the heart could ever incline a sinner's heart to seek salvation. No amount of human persuasion or even hardship could bring a lost sinner to seek and to serve the Lord. No amount of striving by works could get a sin-stained soul to Heaven, and no mere ceremony could expiate guilt.

'Thy will be done': it is a way of saying, 'Lord, we accept and acknowledge that only Thy way can bring salvation to pass, for this is *Thy* work, not ours, and Thy blessing is essential.'

Wait, O my soul, your Maker's will:
Tumultuous passions, all be still,
Nor let a murmuring thought arise:
His ways are just, His counsels wise.

4 Fourthly, in this petition we promise to *submit ourselves to God's will.* We say, 'Lord, Thy will and rule is laid out in Thy Word, and I submit myself to it, yield myself to all Thy commands, and renounce my own ideas, and my selfish ambitions, to make the cause of Christ my chief aim and pleasure.'

5 Fifthly, in the petition, 'Thy will be done,' we pray for the enlargement of God's kingdom. God has said that it is His will to save a great host of people, and so we pray that many more may be gathered in. We intercede for lost souls, and pray that we may see more and more of God's sovereign mercy operating in the lives of those around us.

6 Sixthly, this petition is also a triumphant affirmation that the will of God *must* prevail over all the activities of Satan. God's will, by contrast with the will of the enemy of souls, will surely prevail. The devil has a will also, but it is supported by vastly inferior power, and he is already a defeated, wandering, vagabond fiend. He has only a temporary opportunity to rampage around this present earth doing his worst, but Christ will finally throw him down. Therefore, when we say, 'Thy will be done,' we affirm the inferiority of the evil one and his utter inadequacy ever to lift himself up against the omnipotent God. We declare that his will is already defeated and can only be expressed for a space of time. 'Thy will be done' proclaims the everlasting superiority and victory of the Lord, and worships Him as Conqueror.

* * *

It is a great shame that the Lord's Prayer – for many believers – is only ever recited or read through quickly, so that the full significance of each petition is lost in the flow of thought. To include, at intervals, several aspects of the third petition in our prayers will help us to trust the Lord and pledge ourselves more firmly to Him.

7

The Fourth Petition
'Give us this day our daily bread'

Daily Needs of Body and Soul

'Day by day the manna fell:
Help me learn this lesson well;
So, by constant mercy fed,
Grant me, Lord, my daily bread.'
Josiah Conder

I F WE WANT to know about priorities in prayer, the teaching
of Christ may surprise us. It is a striking fact that out of seven
petitions in the Lord's Prayer, only one refers directly to physical matters – 'Give us this day our daily bread.' We learn from this
that we are to give more attention to spiritual matters, such as the
cause of Christ and personal spiritual advance, than to bodily needs.
Nevertheless, we are to appreciate that our bodily needs are supplied by God, and we are to bring them before Him.

People are often puzzled at the fact that bodily needs are put before forgiveness. One suggested explanation is that once the prayer has turned to subjective, personal needs, it rises from the lesser to the greater spiritual needs, such as pardon and sanctifying grace. Other teachers put the order down to the fact that bodily survival precedes the survival of the soul. Still others say that bread is mentioned before forgiveness so that the whole prayer shall begin and end with spiritual matters, although it is doubtful that such an ornamental consideration would have been in the mind of the Lord.

One commentator from long ago said that when he first began to study the Lord's Prayer he regarded it as a very short prayer, but by the time he came to the fourth petition, he decided it was so profound that it would take a lifetime to pray. The petition for daily bread is an example of the depth of this wonderful prayer. In the Bible, bread is often put for any kind of crop or fruit. In the time of Christ, Roman culture included under the term 'bread' not only foods, but clothing too. So it was a very broad word, used in a general as well as in a specific sense.

The petition says, '*Give us* this day.' On the authority of Jesus Christ we may come and pray for all things essential to the life of the body, remembering that we cannot pay God, the Supreme Provider, Who gives all things as gifts. To keep this in mind helps us in character development, because people who are deeply conscious that they receive a free and gracious supply from God, cannot easily be mean and niggardly. This petition, therefore, serves as an antidote to meanness. The rule of Christ is – 'Freely ye have received, freely give.'

1. 'Bread' Signifies Necessity

What scale of material benefit should we pray for? The answer lies in the word *bread*. Although it stands here for all bodily needs, yet it describes a very *basic* commodity. We ought to pray only for those things which are reasonable and necessary. The Lord's Prayer provides no warrant or right to pray for luxuries and extravagances, so we will not pray for a Rolls Royce, or any other unnecessary, expensive and excessive things. We should not pray for an unnecessarily splendid home, but we do have warrant to pray for what is reasonable and will bring glory to God. If the Lord should provide more than the level of provision for which we pray, we will need to seek grace to manage that blessing in the right way. By using the word *bread*, this pattern petition sets a standard for our lives, and limits our desires. We are forced to ask ourselves – Is it necessary? Is it reasonable? Is it God-honouring? Is it only self-serving? Is it wanted out of covetousness or vainglory? Is it stealing from stewardship? Will it set a bad example to others? The very fact that our significant bodily needs must be brought before the Lord in prayer, is surely a deterrent to covetousness. When tempted, we say, 'I cannot pray for that, because I know it fails the standard.'

To look at this another way, we note that bread has a most important but restricted purpose. As a rule it is not made the high point of a meal in terms of flavour. We acknowledge that the flavour of bread may be appreciated, but that is not its greatest attribute, nor is bread enthusiastically sought after for the sake of its appearance. Bread is valued on account of its practical benefits, providing energy and strength for life and work. In line with this, the kind of 'bread' we are to pray for is that which is useful and profitable. Whenever we pray for bodily provisions we ask – Is this helpful to me in my life and service for the Lord, so that I may more effectively carry out all the tasks He has commanded me to do in business and family life? We may be looking for a house, and questions will arise – Is it in the right place for Christian service? Is it excessive – beyond what is necessary? Is it going to spoil my Christian life and detract from my spiritual usefulness in any way?

Bread, we have mentioned, is not for show. The bodily provisions for which we pray will not be for pride and ostentation. We do not have authority to pray for things that will make us appear better than other people, and cause us to be admired. Certainly bread is not consumed in order to get drunk, and therefore we should not pray for things to gratify the unending human appetite for excessive pleasure.

2. Bread Signifies Daily Reliance

Bread also reminds us of our human vulnerability and dependence. In those days, when there were no modern food-storage facilities, bread was never taken for granted. Crops were subject to weather conditions, and they could not absolutely count on having an adequate harvest. We must learn to pray as people who are still vulnerable and in need of the providence, protection and blessing of God. We should not count on these things without prayer.

By nature, fallen human beings are full of pride, but to pray for the most basic needs of life helps to keep us humble. Prayer for daily provisions including needs such as jobs and income, coupled with daily thanksgiving to God, not only regulates greed but also suppresses pride.

Why are we taught to pray for the bodily needs of this particular day? The Greek term translated 'this day' means either – from day to day, or, for the coming day. We must therefore pray for our bodily provisions for the immediate future; for the short term. Perhaps this wording is intended to confront our tendency to over-provide for ourselves, and to be concerned about life's precise direction and security into the distant future. This is not how this prayer wants us to live. Of course, there is a place for making proper provision for the future, but not excessively, because that is against the principle implied here. Obviously if we can, we provide so that no one who is dependent upon us will become destitute, but we should be more concerned about the work of the Gospel than for over-providing for ourselves for years to come. Some believers invest all their resources for the last years of their lives, which is surely contrary to any reasonable standard of faith and commitment. Ours is a life of trust in God, and we are not meant to be *so* secure that we do not have to trust Him.

To be obliged to pray for things from day to day, or constantly, reinforces the humbling process already referred to. Nebuchadnezzar built Babylon to massive proportions, his palace and his city walls being so solid and durable in appearance that the city projected an air of invincibility. Wherever he looked, the emperor saw scenes of grandeur and security. But it had a disastrous effect upon him, and he began to speak of what he had built by the might of his power and for the glory of his majesty. The Lord prevents His people from coming to this level of self-reliance by requiring them to depend on Him from day to day for bodily and spiritual needs. We shall never feel absolutely safe in our own strength or incapable of falling while we sincerely pray, 'Give us this day . . .'

It may be quite hard to pray for our daily bodily needs if we are surrounded by plenty. If we have the money for necessities, and cannot see any reason why our supplies should cease, it will seem unnecessary to come before the Lord praying that food will be on the table tomorrow. It will certainly seem hard to pray with feeling, because there is no pressing need. In such circumstances, as far as material needs are concerned, it may be better to change the nature of our prayer into most earnest thanksgiving, never forgetting to render thanks. We must acknowledge that God is the source and fountain of all things, and that He cares for us.

Bodily needs include health and vigour, for these may fail very suddenly, and should never be taken for granted. Health and vigour are not the same, for someone may be in reasonably good health, and yet lack the physical and emotional energy to engage meaningfully in the Lord's work in their congregation. We should also pray for mental acumen for Bible study and witness, and if we lack fellowship, we should pray for friends, for this is also a basic human need. We are made relational beings, in the image of the Tri-une God, and we need the encouragement (not to mention the mutual admonition) of companionship.

3. Bread Represents Spiritual Provisions

The term *bread* also includes spiritual provisions, for did not the Saviour say, 'I am the bread of life'? Salvation is pictured by bread in many respects. Bread is supplied to the body from outside, creatures being unable to produce their own sustenance from within themselves. Similarly, salvation and spiritual life must be freely given by the work of the Spirit. The righteousness of Jesus Christ also must be *imputed* to us.

Bread, though ultimately given by God, has to be harvested, milled and baked, and so it is with salvation. If we do not seek the Lord, we shall not find Him; if we do not repent, we shall not be forgiven; if we do not yield to Him, we shall never be governed by Him.

Bread has a fairly immediate effect, for within hours after ingestion new energy is available. Salvation is the same, for when the seeking soul sincerely pleads for forgiveness and new life, then those blessings come certainly and soon. Bread illustrates conversion as a 'crisis event' rather than a lifelong process.

We have already noted that bread is not wonderful to look at, and even in this respect it pictures the Bread of Life and the way of salvation. Although the Saviour is glorious in the heavens, eternal and almighty, yet when we look to Him for salvation we see Him humiliated, suffering and dying on a cross. At Calvary He wore no grand regalia, and in those hours manifested no outward signs of power and authority, but His work was the greatest accomplishment in the history of time, and to eat of Him is to be filled with eternal life.

Bread, of course, pictures that daily light from the Word, and sanctifying grace. A single day missed brings a time of relative darkness, coldness and weakness. The pithy words of Puritan John Trapp on the Lord's Prayer challenge believers to pray this fourth petition in the right spirit. He speaks of *spiritual* bread.

'We have not a bit of bread of our own earning, but must get our living by begging. He that shall go to God as the Prodigal did, saying, "Give me the portion that falleth to me," shall receive but the wages of sin. Beggars also pay no debts, but acknowledge their insufficiency, and speak supplications in humble terms, as broken men. So must we. And because beggars must be no choosers, ask as our Saviour here directs, for downright household bread. A godly man asks but for the bread of the day, enough to bring him home to his Father's house.'

8

The Fifth Petition

'And forgive us our debts'

The Way and the Terms of Repentance

> 'Lord, I confess to Thee
> Sadly my sin;
> All I have done and said,
> All I have been.
> Purge Thou my sin away,
> Wash Thou my soul this day,
> Lord, make me clean.'
>
> *Horatius Bonar*

WE SHOULD first notice the opening word of this fifth petition – 'And'. This little word is of rather obvious significance in that it links this petition with the preceding one, both sharing the words 'this day'. Therefore, we should read – 'this day . . . forgive us our debts.' Daily repentance is a most crucial component in the believer's prayer life. To omit this, or to allow it to degenerate into a few words, is to risk all assured spiritual experience. We may truly be converted; we may be safe for all eternity, but without *regular* forgiveness, we shall soon suffer reversals in sanctification, the loss of answered prayer, and the waning of spiritual instrumentality. We shall certainly lose that lively interaction between the Lord and ourselves in our lives, our reaching up to Him in satisfying daily communion, and His reaching down to us with clear interventions in our lives. We may feel happy and at peace, but only with the peace of self-delusion. Any sense of calm will only conceal the fact that meaningful communion with God has ceased, and the Christian life become a kind of sleepwalk.

No Repentance – No Sanctification

Think how the neglect of daily repentance halts the process of sanctification. If there is no seeking of forgiveness, there will be no preparatory self-examination either, and if there is no daily review of heart and conduct, sin will get a better hold. After a few days we will become noticeably worse in the restraining of our typical sins, and those people around us in our home, or place of study or business will see that our behaviour has deteriorated. They may see, for example, that we are not reacting to problems with calm and courtesy, but with irritability and selfishness, and our testimony will be ruined.

Without daily self-examination and repentance our consciences will quickly lose their sensitivity and become hardened, and our spiritual tastes will also be soured. Pride and hypocrisy in particular are bound to come creeping back in. Furthermore, without daily repentance, our other prayers will no longer be answered. If we have neglected daily repentance, we should jolt ourselves back to life with the following thoughts:–

Think of what you could have prayed for. Think of the people for whom you could have interceded. Think of the unmistakable interventions by God that would have been seen in your life. But you did not repent for several days, and your facility for prayer was forfeited. God will not act like the indulgent parent who spoils his children with good things no matter how badly they behave. The sincere seeking of forgiveness, after due self-examination, is not a burdensome, tiresome practice, but one which brings us immense blessing.

The Meaning of 'Debts'

The Lord used the word 'debts' in the pattern prayer – 'Forgive us our *debts*.' It is clear that this refers to sins, because when this prayer was taught in another place (recorded in *Luke 11*) He used the word 'sins' instead of 'debts', and words are important. The word 'debt' reminds us that whenever we sin we deny the Lord His due or right. Right-
eousness is God's right, not only something He desires. It is His right to have our worship, our obedience, our love, our service, and our holi-
ness. Our sin incurs a debt because God has given us so many things, including life itself, and we have taken those things, used them for our own enjoyment and advantage, made no adequate return, and offended in evil thoughts, words and deeds. As believers, our debt has been paid by Christ, Who bore the punishment of sin for us, but ongoing sin continues to be viewed as a debt, which must be cleared by repentance.

> There are so many sins that if we do not seek cleansing every day the mountain of guilt will rise so high that we may be alto-
gether swept away from Christian exper-
ience and delivered up to be severely chastised.

In the Lord's Prayer the plural is used – 'forgive us our *debts*.' We commit many sins, and we cannot remember them all, even when repenting on a daily basis. The Lord, in His kindness, does not require us to mention them all, and if we were to try, repentance would be a horrible and a gruelling ordeal. But we must try to remember the chief ones, examining our hearts and lamenting some of them. We commit sins of word, thought and deed. We are guilty of sins of omission and sins of commission. There are sins that have festered and smouldered in the mind, and there are sins of impulse. There are sins of envy, of hate, and of injury to others. There are so many different sins, and in some way and at some time and in some shape we are guilty of them all. There are so many sins that if we do not seek cleansing every day the mountain of guilt will rise so high that we may be altogether swept away from Christian experience and delivered up to be severely chastised.

The Meaning of 'Forgive'

The Lord's Prayer reads – 'And *forgive* us our debts.' The Greek word translated 'forgive' means to 'send forth' or 'send away'. We say, 'Lord, send away my sin, take it away so that it will no longer stand against me. Take it away so that my record is no longer besmirched and stained. Take it away so that I may be regarded as though I had not sinned. Take away the guilt, and also break the hold and the habit of the sin. Help me to get rid of it so that it will not plague my life any more.'

To ask for the sin to be sent away must include an appeal for help to overcome the sin in future. 'Send away' refers not only to the *guilt*, but also to the *act*, and no repentance is genuine if it does not include a pledge or undertaking or longing to do better in future. It is not enough to say, 'Lord, forgive my guilt,' when we have no intention of fighting the sin. We pray, 'Lord, help me to expel this sin; give me the strength to overcome it; grant me a hatred of it; give new life to my conscience, to warn me when this temptation draws near.' *Psalm 51* is a model prayer of repentance, balancing deep and genuine remorse with strong pleas for help in future holiness.

Remedies for Loss of Conviction

At a practical level, people often ask if repentance, to be valid, requires a deep sense of conviction or shame. Should we *feel* sinful? Believers also ask what they should do if there is no recollection of sin. They go before the Lord to repent, but cannot remember what their sins are. They can think of one or two, but the activity is hardly serious. May we suggest a number of remedies or helps for dealing with such problems.

1 First is the principle of James – 'If any of you lack wisdom, let him ask of God.' Pray for light and conviction; for a clear view of yourself and how you appear to the Holy God. The desired insight may not come at once, in which case you will have to repent daily without it, but continue asking that God will give a keener awareness of sin and its ugliness. Do not desire a crushing, overwhelming sense of sinfulness, but a clear, shame-producing awareness. Excessive conviction easily takes the form of emotional self-indulgence, which is mere sentimentality. Make Charles Wesley's prayer your own:

> *That blessèd sense of guilt impart,*
> *And then remove the load;*
> *Trouble, then wash the troubled heart*
> *In the atoning blood.*

2 The second remedy for lack of conviction or shame is to spend time thinking about God's attributes and perfections, and His great kindness toward us. *Isaiah 6* teaches us that when the glory of the Lord is seen then we fall before Him saying, 'Woe is me! for I am undone; because I am a man of unclean lips.' The glory of God lights up all our imperfections. In private prayer and reflection make much of praising and thanking God for His infinite power, majesty and wisdom. Praise Him for His wonderful ways, His

lovingkindness, His faithfulness, and especially His infinite and wonderful purity and perfection.

If you think that you are not eloquent enough to do justice to the character of God, then go to a scripture that will do it for you. Select a psalm, or a great doxology from one of Paul's epistles, or perhaps the great exalting, opening passage of an epistle like *Ephesians*. Read each sentiment and then close your eyes and praise Him and thank Him for them. This may well provoke your conscience and your sense of need for His great mercy. Then add to that a review of your privileges, and see the ingratitude, disrespect and arrogance inherent in sin.

3 A third remedy for lack of conviction is to be seen in the structure of the Lord's Prayer. Do not necessarily begin your time of prayer with repentance. Although it is a good start, it is not an essential beginning, for in the Lord's Prayer we give praise first, then we pray for the cause and the advance of the kingdom, which undoubtedly includes intercession for others. As we pray in some detail for selected relatives, colleagues, fellow students, neighbours, preachers, missionaries, sick, needy and the oppressed, our spiritual senses are often aroused, and then we are more able to recall and regret our sins. Sympathetic, unselfish prayer kindles gratitude, faith and love, so that the heart co-operates better in prayers of repentance.

4 A fourth remedy for low conviction or little sense of shame is to stimulate the desire for forgiveness by referring to it more frequently. For a few days, in everything you pray for, mention forgiveness. As you ask for different blessings say, 'Lord, my prayer can only be heard for this person, if I am right with Thee, so forgive my sins. I repent of this, and of this, and of this.' This may be asked alongside every petition, and the ability to feel conviction may be rekindled.

5 A fifth remedy is to give more time to self-examination. It may help to do this for several days by 'instalments', stopping to reflect on your need for progress in holiness several times in the course of your prayers. Spend a few moments each time examining your heart and thinking about what you have done and the kind of person you have been. Think also of what you have not done. As you think of your omissions, conviction often awakens. Think also of your neglect of witness. Think of your failure in showing kindness and supportiveness to those who should have received it. It may be that the church has greatly needed your participation and you have withheld it while chasing after your own interests. Bring such sins into focus, and think, too, of the so-called 'heart sins', or sins of *condition*, such as pride and selfishness.

6 If such measures do not bring the conscience to life, then this sixth remedy may help. Think of those conspicuous past sins for which you have already been forgiven. You should not repent of them again, but thank God that He forgave those sins when you called upon Him and submitted to Him. Think of how much you owe, marvel at how patient He has been towards you. Think of sins that went on for months, even for years, before you repented and mended your ways. Think of those massive debts from the past, those conspicuous, glaring sins, and thank Him until the heart melts and the tears flow. Then greater conviction for present sins may be re-ignited.

7 A final necessary course of action to take when conviction seems to fail is to repent with the mind, without waiting for feeling. Take the measures suggested to make repentance a matter of the heart, but in the period before conviction returns, repent intellectually, acknowledging your dependence on the blood of Christ, and mercy alone. Do not be greatly inhibited by lack of feeling. Repent in whatever way you can, because although feelings of conviction

are a normal part of repentance they are not absolutely essential. If you repent with care and with some degree of detail, though feelings may be dormant, they will in due course be revived, and God will deepen your concerns.

The Condition for Forgiveness

When a major political figure repeatedly committed grievous moral sin and it came into the full light of public knowledge, a famous Christian preacher appeared on television saying that he had forgiven him. But the politician's sin was against God, and there had been no indication that he had repented to Him. The preacher had no right to absolve him from blame. We should not take it upon ourselves to forgive those who sin *against God.* That is God's prerogative. Sometimes one hears that a church has had to discipline a member who has fallen into serious sin, and some misguided soul has said, 'I will bypass the judgement of the church, because I forgive him.'

Forgiving our debtors means forgiving those who have sinned against us, injuring us perhaps by some offence. To forgive means that we show no contempt, hostility or coolness, banishing from our minds resentment or hurt. We do not adopt an unco-operative spirit, or nurture any desire for the offender's hurt or undoing. If the offence is moderate, we should forgive even in the absence of visible regret or apology.

One or more of the following attitudes may hinder us extending forgiveness to a person who offends against us. We may want bitterness to persist. We may be unprepared to build a bridge, or even to be affable. We may have a proud spirit – so proud that anyone who wounds us can never be forgiven by us. We may possess a fault-finding, critical spirit, and this will make us very unsympathetic and judgemental. If we fail to take a right attitude toward an offender quickly, bitterness may be compacted and an exaggerated view of the offence nurtured in our minds. We may be disinclined to forgive because the offender is not important to us, or because there is no natural 'chemistry' or affinity. There may be additional resentment on our part because the offender has at some time laid bare some wrong conduct on our part, so that our pride and indignation has been inflamed. However, we are warned that if we ignore God and show no forgiving spirit we will forfeit God's forgiveness. So firm is God in this matter that the pattern prayer requires us to actually state that we will forgive others.

Normally those who offend against us should acknowledge their wrong and show some regret, but forgiveness should be extended unasked if the matter is not great, because 'charity shall cover the multitude of sins.' Furthermore, this is how God graciously deals with us, overlooking countless faults of which we are unaware. Equally, forgiveness should be given without repentance if the offence was provoked or compacted by us. The Saviour's commandment is that His people should love one another, and Paul is inspired to exhort – 'Let your moderation be known unto all men.' Moderation is magnanimity and generosity of spirit, or sweet reasonableness. We are instructed to be 'kind one to another, tenderhearted, forgiving one another'. We are to be constantly 'forbearing one another, and forgiving one another'. If the offence is an offence directly against God or His Truth, then it must be repented of to Him, but personal offences between people should be readily forgiven.

We repeat the observation that in our pattern prayer the Lord requires us to state in words an undertaking to forgive others. If this is a required, verbal clause in our repentance, then it is obviously of immense importance.

9

The Sixth Petition

'And lead us not into temptation'

Preparing for the Battle

'I want a godly fear,
A quick-discerning eye,
That looks to Thee when sin is near,
And sees the tempter fly;
A spirit still prepared,
And armed with jealous care,
For ever standing on its guard,
And watching unto prayer.'

Charles Wesley

THE SIXTH and seventh petitions, though linked, should
ideally be seen separately – 'And lead us not into temptation, but deliver us from evil.' Though disarmingly simple
in sense, they give great insight into how we may advance in personal holiness. It appears that the first petition is negative and the
second more positive, but there is a better way of distinguishing
between them. 'Lead us not into temptation' is about preparing for

the daily battle with sin, whereas 'Deliver us from evil' is a plea to God to use all means to correct, keep and deliver us once we are in the thick of the battle. The distinction between the two petitions is of preparation and implementation.

First, we shall explore the first part – 'Lead us not into temptation.' We realise that God is never the author of evil, and James warns – 'Let no man say when he is tempted, I am tempted of God: for God cannot be tempted with evil, neither tempteth he any man.' This petition cannot therefore mean, 'Lord, do not lead us into sin,' as though He would do so without this prayer. It is certainly true that God may take away His restraining hand so that we stumble into sin because of our pride and foolishness, but He never leads His people into temptation. This is a prayer of acknowledgement that we cannot go through life and fight against sin without God's blessing and power. We shall look at eight kinds of help which we pray for when we say, 'Lead us not into temptation.'

1. A Prayer for Vigilance

First, we are saying, 'Lord, I am vulnerable and weak; keep me alert and vigilant in the battle against sin.' We must prepare for the day in prayer, because the devil may hurl many evil thoughts into our minds. He will not necessarily tempt us with gross evil, because this may alarm us and drive us to the Lord. He is more likely to begin his campaign by introducing to our mind smaller temptations, perhaps urging us to react badly to situations. His method will be characterised by subtlety and cunning, and he will probably ensure that all sinful urgings are accompanied by self-justifying reasoning. 'Be vigilant,' writes the apostle Peter, 'because your adversary the devil, as a roaring lion, walketh about, seeking whom he may devour.'

There is a Pharisee in every person, who wants to say, 'I can cope, I can do it.' We may never actually articulate these thoughts, but self-sufficiency creates in us a strange complacency, as though we have conquered many sins before and will fairly easily do so again. 'Lead us not into temptation' is a way of saying, 'Lord, I am not sufficient for this warfare. Do not allow pride and self-confidence to delude me, so that I imagine I can withstand temptation in my own strength.'

2. A Prayer for an Alert Conscience

Secondly, 'Lead us not into temptation' is a way of asking for a tender conscience. We are not yet fully in the battle, for we have not launched out into the day. An important preparatory request is – 'Lord, grant me a tender conscience, that it may be stirred as soon as temptation draws near. Deliver me from sailing through the day unaware of the sins I am slipping into. Grant me a conscience that will spark to life and warn me, even painfully if necessary, when I am heading into sin.' We must pray daily for a lively conscience, and when we do we receive it, and we are warned and cautioned about our words and deeds, we no longer go blindly into the battle. Charles Wesley's great hymn expresses the need:

> I want a principle within
> Of jealous, godly fear;
> A sensibility of sin,
> A pain to feel it near.

> I want the first approach to feel
> Of pride, or fond desire;
> To catch the wandering of my will,
> And quench the kindling fire.

> That I from Thee no more may part,
> No more Thy goodness grieve,
> The filial awe, the feeling heart,
> The tender conscience, give.

Quick as the glancing of an eye,
O God, my conscience make!
Awake my soul, when sin is nigh,
And keep it still awake.

3. A Prayer for Divine Guidance

Thirdly, in this petition we are asking that God will keep alive within us a keen desire for His guidance in all the major issues of life. It is another way of saying, 'Lord, when I am confronted by major decisions and possibilities, prevent me from rushing on and doing things for myself, in my own way, so moving into sinful mistakes. Whether it is a major decision about work, family life, study, financial commitment or even leisure, prevent me, Lord, from making it thoughtlessly. Help me to ever see myself as Thy servant, under Thy direction in all things. Keep alive within me a sense of duty to Thee and Thy cause.'

The moment we behave as 'free agents' who can do what they like as long as it does not involve serious sin, then we are on the road to error. Soon we take decisions for our own benefit all the time. This prayer of preparation asks to be constantly reminded that we are children of God, under His rule and direction, and that in all the great affairs and decisions of life we must seek to honour Him.

4. A Prayer for Sound Ministry

Fourthly, in this petition we are praying that the Lord may keep us (or lead us) under sound ministry. Wherever our lot be cast, uppermost in our minds should be our need of continuing biblical ministry. Some Christians neglect this, imagining that sound biblical ministry grows on trees, but we live in a spiritually decadent age. Many, sadly, have moved home and job, and the last thing they have considered is their access to a faithful church and ministry. 'Lead us not into temptation,' is another way of saying, 'Lord, give us ministry that will feed us from the Word, build up our souls, challenge our hearts, and keep us from backsliding.' The blessing of sound ministry should never be taken for granted.

5. A Prayer for Victory over Besetting Sins

Fifthly, this petition is a prayer to know our particular, personal weaknesses, so that we may set a special watch over them, and not place ourselves in the pathway of sin. What are my particular weaknesses? All believers have their own besetting sin-tendency. It may be pride or vainglory, or the curse of a tendency to dishonesty, or laziness and love of ease, or an excessive love of pleasure, or covetousness, or a serious lack of faith that produces endless fear and worry, or self-pity, or grumbling and complaining, or gossip and constant criticism, or foul temper or an unrestrained tongue. We must surely know ourselves and the weaknesses which bring us down. Like an alcoholic who must not go near a drop of liquor, or any other former addict who should keep well away from his old ways, we must know ourselves, recognise our failings, and take care that we do not put ourselves in positions where these may be exploited by Satan. 'Lead me not into temptation' is a prayer for help in being on guard, and watchful about specific sins. It is also a way of saying – 'Keep me aware of my pre-conversion sins: those things which drove and ruled me before.' Old sins very often attempt a come-back as the Christian life goes on.

6. A Prayer for Hatred of Sin

Sixthly, this petition, 'Lead us not into temptation,' puts into our mouths a firm declaration of our opposition to sin, and a prayer to be given an increased hatred of sin. We tell the Lord we do not want it, we hate it, and it is our bitter enemy, and we plead for greater loathing of it. It is vital that we should take this stance. The trouble with sin is that it can seem so powerfully attractive, whether we are drawn into thinking of possessions, or of triumphs for vainglory. Even the venting of an angry, vengeful spirit can give rise to great, if perverted, satisfaction, and no one would deny the compelling attractiveness of excessive ease and pleasure. Any number of attractive and yet sinful thoughts may fill our minds, and so we ask, 'Lord, give me a greater horror of sin, that I may hate it more than I have ever loved it and that I may not want to commit it. Help me to see its ugliness and offensiveness to Thee. Help me to see the damage it does. Lord, give me a clear view of sin.' If we relax our suspicion and disgust over sin we forfeit a key piece of armour to protect against it. 'Lead us not into temptation' says, 'Give me an abhorrence of sin, so that I recoil from it.'

7. A Prayer for Love of Godliness

Seventhly, this petition asks for the preservation of a godly life, and a greater love of holiness and righteousness. We pray, 'Help me to love Christian character and conduct. Help me to delight in the law of God after the inward man.' The Saviour said – 'Blessed are they which do hunger and thirst after righteousness' – and so we plead for a real and deep appreciation of good character and Christian virtues. To some extent we can help promote these in ourselves. Do we not value very deeply many other Christians? Do we not sometimes stand amazed at their unselfish character and tireless labours? We should be melted in praise to God for His handiwork, and desire it for ourselves. We should ask God for the same attributes and virtues. We may pray – 'Lord, my foolish mind settles upon all sorts of trivial and passing things, appreciating them far more than they deserve. Help me to bring my appreciation of godliness to a much higher level, that this may motivate me to advance.'

8. A Prayer Against Excess Prosperity

Eighthly, 'Lead us not into temptation' is a prayer that we shall not to be brought into comforts, triumphs and accomplishments that are too much for us to handle. We say, 'Lord, protect me from being flattered, rewarded, and over-provided for by this passing world. Do not let me be weighed down by things in this world which will pull down my soul.' This may be the opposite of what we are inclined to pray for. We may prefer to ask for promotion, or more money, and for greater ease and comfort, but 'Lead us not into temptation' asks the very opposite. 'Lead us not into comfortable complacency, so that we become spoiled, worldly, and proud, and lead us not into the rat-race of seeking our worldly good to the detriment of the spiritual life.'

We pray, 'Lord, we will accept Thy judgement, and accept Thy providence. Whatever Thou dost give us, we will accept. Lord, only deliver us from ever being brought into a position from which we shall fall. Lead us not into temptation.'

10

'But deliver us from evil'

In the Thick of the Battle

'If to the right or left I stray,
That moment, Lord, reprove;
And let me weep that hour away,
For having grieved Thy love.'
Charles Wesley

'LEAD US not into temptation, but *deliver us from evil.*' The second of these linked petitions may also be translated, 'Deliver us from *the* evil', or as Calvin insisted, 'from the evil one', referring to Satan. Many old divines prefer 'evil' to be understood as encompassing the world and the flesh as well as the devil. Temptation will come, and residual sin will constantly be stirred up within us, for although we have a new nature, we still have the old one, albeit subdued, and it will rise up and assert itself. In the first of these two petitions we prayed to God to strengthen and prepare us, but now we view ourselves as in the midst of the battle, projecting ourselves into our waking, working day, and we cry out to be protected and delivered. What exactly are we to pray for? Here we suggest three possible topics for prayer, all reasonably implied by the words – 'Deliver us from evil.'

1. Help at the Vital Moment of Temptation

First, 'Deliver us from evil' is a prayer for *determination* to mortify and correct sin. We ask also for help to expel from our minds wrong thoughts should they invade. When things which we do not need or should not have, or which will waste our time, or make us vain, begin to seem attractive and desirable, then we will need the strength to put them out of our lives. James says that – 'Every man is tempted, when he is drawn away of his own lust, and enticed.' This is the point at which we most need to resist temptation, quelling all desire to succumb, and turning our minds to something better. We must pray for an implacable determination to wrest ourselves away from the offensive idea.

It is a tragedy when the Lord's people become influenced by the ideas of the so-called holiness movement, which claims that believers need not fight to resist sin. They need only to fix their eye on the cross, or on Christ, or 'abide in Him' by some act of will or of mystical focus, and God will do it all for them. The opposite is the truth – that when temptation comes we should muster our determination and strength to prayerfully and actively resist and fight against the sin.

2. Help to Keep Up Spiritual Duties

Secondly, we should pray to be kept from any temptation or pressure that may arise when in the thick of the struggle, to give up and abandon our spiritual duties and our concern for a good witness in the sight of unbelievers. In the hour of need we require a strong sense of duty, gratitude and faith so that we will not put off praise, prayer, attention to God's Word and testimony. Whatever troubles may swirl round us, we want to be held and kept faithful. So we pray, 'When I am tempted to despondency, help me to maintain faith and dependence, and to pray through every situation. When preoccupied by many things, help me to witness. Deliver me also from unreasonableness, and all other unworthy reactions in the hour of temptation and satanic trial.'

3. Help to Accept Correction

Thirdly, 'Deliver us from evil' is a prayer asking God to use any necessary means to discipline us when we sin, and make us better people. It includes the prayer – 'Lord, chastise me as necessary; punish me and correct me as the perfect Father, and I promise to accept it and heed it.' All believers need a form of chastisement from the Lord from time to time, when a painful or restricting experience may pull them up short and make them examine their life. In this petition we promise to heed and not to resent God's dealings with us. *Hebrews 12.5* quotes *Proverbs* in the exhortation: 'My son, despise not thou the chastening of the Lord, nor faint when thou art rebuked of him.'

In this petition we also make ourselves open to any correction which the Lord may channel through fellow believers. We say, 'Lord, when my fellow believers chastise me, may I respect and value what they say, hearing it in the right spirit. Let them not withhold their words of caution and reproof. Give me the humility to listen, even today and this week, and to mend my ways.' In the words of the psalmist we pray, 'Let the righteous smite me; it shall be a kindness: and let him reprove me; it shall be an excellent oil.' Isaac Watts expressed these words in his hymn version of *Psalm 141* –

> *O may the righteous, when I stray,*
> *See and reprove my wandering way.*

All these desires and prayers are surely suggested by the petition – 'Deliver us from evil.'

A summary chart of the 'departments' of prayer derived from the Lord's Prayer

Adoration of God

Affirmation

Thanksgiving   ⟶   an implicit part of every department, as each petition also presents a cause for profound gratitude and praise

Intercession

Dedication

Spiritual and Bodily Needs

Repentance

Prayer for Help in Holiness

Submission and Glorying in the Lord and His Eternal Plan

11

The Doxology
'For thine is the kingdom, and the power, and the glory, for ever. Amen.'

He Must Have the Glory

'Thine, then, for ever be
Glory and power divine;
The sceptre, throne and majesty
Of Heaven and earth are Thine.'
James Montgomery

A T THE CONCLUSION of this magnificent pattern prayer we are given a final affirmation of the ownership and power of God, from which we draw eight observations that inspire trust, shape our spiritual outlook, and suggest what we should have in mind when we pray these great words. It must be said that if these words do not shape our attitude to life also, then we can hardly pray them with sincerity. How often is this prayer recited, we wonder, by those upon whom it has no guiding influence? May the Lord help us to take them as a policy for life, as well as a prayer.

1. His Property – for His Pleasure

'Thine is the kingdom' affirms that our church, the Scriptures, our eternal home, and the redeemed host are all His property, and He has the right to dispose all things according to His pleasure. Everything we do in the life and worship of our church, is for the owner's pleasure, and not primarily for ours. If we hold office, it is delegated office, and we should carry out His commands as those who will one day render an account of our conduct.

'Thine is the kingdom' – also reminds us that we must defer to Him in all things and yield ourselves up to Him. In no department of our lives should we ever say, 'This is mine and I will do as I choose.' Every decision we take of any consequence in our personal lives or in our church life is to be taken in this light – What should I do to obey and please the Lord? Always ask – How do I fit into the scheme of God Who owns the whole church, and my soul? What service should I be undertaking? We should never ask – Will I enjoy this avenue of service? Will it suit me? Will I find it convenient? If God equips and gives the opportunity, then surely we must do it. If God calls, we must follow; after all, we and the kingdom are His property.

2. All Are Under His Power

'Our God can do anything,' we say in these closing words. With ease He will consummate His purposes and bring His kingdom in. He will cause His will to be done on earth as it is in Heaven, converting sinners, calling them out of the world, bringing their hearts to life, and bringing them to Himself. He will see them all safely into eternity, to stand before Him as redeemed souls, and then, in the last day, will reconstitute their bodies from the dust in glorified form. Because He is all-powerful, when we intercede for lost sinners, for members of our family, for work-place colleagues and many others, we do not do so in a faint-hearted, despairing spirit, because we know that the God on Whom we call can do anything He chooses. The words, 'Thine is the kingdom, and the power and the glory,' when sincerely meant, become the 'vehicle' of faith in which our petitions travel to the highest Heaven.

Whenever we pray we should remember His limitless power. All earthly authorities, whether kings, prime ministers, presidents, managers of units of people, whatever their role, are entirely under His invisible jurisdiction. He can bend their will, change their outlook and their mind as He pleases. Isaiah tells us that God has entirely altered the destiny of nations for the sake of the plan of redemption, and for the protection or gathering in of Zion's children. Even those farthest from the Lord are in His power, and we may be sure that our circumstances will be shaped in answer to prayer so that our testimony will prosper and our spiritual safety be assured. There is no situation beyond the arm of the maker and owner of all, and none can thwart His will and His purpose.

3. Content of Prayer Must Be for Him

The words 'Thine is the kingdom' also monitor the content of our prayers, helping us to emphasise needs which are in the interests of the kingdom, such as the winning of souls, and the sustaining and nourishing of the church. Of course, we may ask for any number of needs, including small matters, but their ultimate objective should be to serve the cause of the King. Do we desire healing from some bodily sickness? Why do we desire this? Is it in order that we may just be free from pain and discomfort, or is it also in order that we may live a better life for Him – perhaps making up time on lost years to love Him, worship Him, witness for Him and bring others to the kingdom? If we find we are asking for things which could not conceivably be said to serve the kingdom but which are solely for ourselves, serve our pride or pleasure, then we should not really be asking for these things. 'Thine is the kingdom' is an affirmation of yieldedness to the Lord, and an acknowledgement that His kingdom should be the sovereign and supreme goal in all the affairs of His subjects.

4. All Credit is the Lord's

'Thine is the kingdom, and the power, and the glory' also says, in effect, 'Lord, I will not take the credit for any blessing or spiritual gain, but I will acknowledge Thee as the source of every benefit and every accomplishment.' If our Sunday School class or Bible class goes well, the power and glory will be entirely seen as the Lord's. As we pray, 'Thine is the kingdom,' we also affirm our dependence upon Him. He brought us into the kingdom by grace and sustains us in it by His power. This prayer keeps us humble, looking to Him for help, and ascribing all success to Him.

5. He is the Source of All Life

'Thine is . . . the power' acknowledges that God alone is the source of life, the only self-existent being in the universe, from Whom all life and good flows. When we think of this it helps us to trust Him. If we pray without having an adequate awareness of how mighty He is we may have trouble believing that answers to prayer shall come to pass. Therefore we include in our prayers – ideally at the beginning and the end – some expression of the mighty power of God. There have been occasions in Bible times when just one tiny shaft of the mighty power of God has been released to fall upon a person, and the effect has been utterly overwhelming. When Christ revealed a little of His glory to Saul of Tarsus he was thrown from his horse and blinded, seeing a light so bright, so dazzling, as to conquer him in both sense and soul. This is the God of power to Whom we pray.

How gently the Lord deals with us today. But one day, when grace has made us ready, we shall see Him, hear His voice as the voice of many waters, and sense His immeasurable majesty and kindness. Then we shall say with full understanding – 'For thine is the kingdom, and the power, and the glory.'

6. Appreciation of Him Never Displaced

'The glory' refers to the excellencies of God in all their fulness, and beyond speech to describe, such as His immensity and infinity, His unchanging spiritual being, His power, knowledge, wisdom, goodness, love, and mercy.

When we mention His glory, we are to appreciate Him, and here is a great weakness in prayer, for we tend to pray, 'Lord, help me in this; Lord, help me in that; Lord, avert this problem; Lord, strengthen me for this trial; provide for my needs; forgive all my sin.' In such praying – valid as it is – appreciation of God is often eclipsed. At times we approach the throne of grace burdened with guilt, grief and trials, and the Lord seems less important than our needs. Whatever the need, appreciation of Him must never be displaced, for glory is due to Him. Is there no praise, no magnifying of His glory, no pausing and realising His majesty? Do we not acknowledge and name His excellencies and His great goodness? The Lord's Prayer teaches us that we should remember His attributes at both the beginning and the end of our prayer, and not simply name them, but appreciate them.

> Is there no praise, no magnifying of His glory, no pausing and realising His majesty? Do we not acknowledge and name His excellencies and His great goodness?

7. The Kingdom is Eternal

The last words of the great pattern prayer are peculiarly stirring and elevating when reflected on. 'Thine is the kingdom, and the power, and the glory, *for ever.*' Think of the eternity of Almighty God. Nothing will ever diminish His Godhead. His holiness and power will never fade, and no power in earth or hell can take away the work He has done in saving souls. The act of regeneration lasts for ever. All that God has done through Christ will stand eternally. The effect and power of the atonement lasts for ever. If He adopts us into His family, we will be in that family for ever.

His love lasts for ever, and never diminishes in any way. We can love very fiercely at times, but our fervour may cool so that the flame needs rekindling. But the pure and deep love of God never fluctuates, never alters, never runs down. Christ's Church shall stand for ever, when made glorious and adapted for glory, and if we settle these facts in our minds, our faith is consolidated, our assurance and security increased, and our sense of privilege and indebtedness intensified.

We are certainly aware that earthly governments do not last for ever. No human authority survives long, for empires fall and businesses either fail or disappear within other enterprises. Mankind struggles desperately to stamp permanence upon its creations, and the great drive to build vast, multinational companies is driven by this 'Babel' spirit as much as by commercial aspiration. We want whatever we do to last. We strain to prove that human accomplishment can stand, and we do everything we can to ensure that it does. But nothing on earth is for ever. By contrast, what privileged people believers are, because our cause and kingdom will endure eternally.

It is sometimes a great temptation for young people who love the Lord, study the Word, strive in holiness, and work to bring others to Christ, when suddenly they learn that an unsaved friend has enjoyed a meteoric rise in his worldly status or career, and has moved into a powerful and significant position in life. The child of God may be tempted to think of the family of faith as being so small, and the devil may taunt and tempt, saying, 'Why aren't you in the larger world accomplishing great things?' But the believer only has to turn to God and say, 'Thine is the kingdom, and the power, and the glory, *for ever*,' and perspective is restored. Some lines in Isaac Watts' paraphrase of *Psalm 73* show how the Christian regains eternal perspective:

> *But in the house of God, their end*
> *Dawned on my mind and stirred my shame;*
> *In slippery places how they stand!*
> *How brief their fortunes and their fame!*

'For ever' speaks about the future when God will end this present age and make all subservient to His own will. No other world order will exist, outside the confines of hell, than that in which God is loved and served and known. Right now we feel overwhelmed by the world's spiritual opposition and apathy, but it will not last for long. We are the privileged ones, secure in the will of God and in His mighty hand.

8. The Essential Amen

The very last word of the pattern prayer is the 'amen', but what is the purpose of this little word? Is it just a way of closing the door and terminating the prayer in due order? Every great piece of music must have a fitting conclusion. If it petered out short of a well-constructed end it would sound wrong and would lack balance. Is this the basis of 'amen' – a correctly punctuated prayer? No, it has far greater significance than that. The meaning, as every reader probably knows, is – 'Lord, let it be so.' Even better in this context is – 'Thine is the kingdom, and the power, and the glory, *so let Thy will stand.*' However, the 'amen' conveys still more. It is a way of saying, 'Lord, I wholeheartedly identify with Thy will; I acknowledge it to be the exclusive, essential, perfect and glorious way, and I therefore marvel at all the objectives of the kingdom, submit to its programme, long for its full accomplishment, and give myself to its study, enjoyment and service. This supreme plan will be my delight and my chief interest. I pledge myself to stand faithful to Thy decisions, and Thy calls.' This is what 'amen' means: it is total identification with God's kingdom purposes. It is the expression of a ransomed soul who worships, admires, accepts, and pledges himself or herself to them. There can be no better or higher way of ending our prayers, because this is the pattern of the Lord.

Key Aspects of Prayer

The following chapters respond to practical questions on —

♦ the nature of 'the prayer of faith'

♦ the reasons for long delays in receiving answers to some prayers

♦ the ministry of intercessory prayer

♦ problems encountered in maintaining prayer

12

Key Aspects of Prayer

What is the Prayer of Faith?

For verily I say unto you, That whosoever shall say unto this mountain, Be thou removed, and be thou cast into the sea; and shall not doubt in his heart, but shall believe that those things which he saith shall come to pass; he shall have whatsoever he saith . . . What things soever ye desire, when ye pray, believe that ye receive them, and ye shall have them (Mark 11.23-24).
And the prayer of faith shall save the sick . . . (James 5.15).

SOME PEOPLE make *faith* a *work*, as though the size of our faith 'qualifies' us to get great answers to prayer. They say, for example, that if our faith is strong enough, every sickness will definitely be healed in answer to prayer. If the sick are not healed, then apparently the fault is in our faith. They teach that the 'prayer of faith' is the ability to convince ourselves that whatever we pray is as good as done, mixing *faith* with *will-power*, which is much nearer to witchcraft than to Christian prayer.

Did the Lord promise that *anything* we pray for will always be granted if only we can succeed in believing that we have already received it? Did James mean to say that so long as we have great faith, prayer for the sick will always result in healing?

Some people are convinced that the answer is – yes. But the literal straining of these promises is superficial and mistaken. It makes the Lord contradict Himself, which He would never do. Furthermore, it is an extremely *Arminian* mistake, because God cannot and would never give away His sovereignty to human beings. All prayer must be subject to the supreme will and wisdom of Almighty God, Who alone knows what is the very best and perfect thing to do in the light of His eternal purposes.

The Moving of Mountains

In *Mark 11.23-24* (quoted at the beginning of this chapter) the Saviour makes several points about prayer. First, He tells us that we should have definite objectives when we pray ('what things soever ye desire'), not praying vaguely without forethought. Secondly, we must really *desire* the things we pray for, which clearly should be significant needs for the advance of the kingdom. The Lord, we remember, was speaking to His disciples to train them to launch and lead the soul-winning work of the coming church age.

Thirdly, we must believe that God is listening and that He will not delay in dealing with our requests, although this does not mean that He will respond to every prayer exactly as we would like, because all the Bible tells us to accept the Lord's wise disposal of the case, such as in the experience of Paul who was not healed of the thorn in his flesh, because God had a purpose in that affliction (*2 Corinthians 12.7-9*).

The casting into the sea of a mountain promised by the Lord is obviously a feat so massive and unnecessary that the disciples would have realised that this was not a literal example, but a picture of mighty things for which we can pray, for the glory of the kingdom. Great schemes for the advance of the kingdom have frequently been accomplished by believers not only in history but in our time, with sites acquired, buildings erected, and people converted in large numbers – all in answer to earnest prayer. We do not know of one literal mountain moved by a prayer, but we know of numerous mountains of obstruction to spiritual advance that have been thrown, as it were, into the sea.

Interestingly, in a similar passage in *Matthew 17.20*, the Saviour says, 'If ye have faith as a grain of mustard seed, ye shall say unto this mountain, Remove hence to yonder place; and it shall remove; and nothing shall be impossible unto you.' Remember, again, that it is the disciples being instructed 'apart' who receive this teaching, and they are being taught to bring about – under the power of the Spirit – a Gospel kingdom, not world-wide geographical recontouring. A most encouraging comment made here by the Lord is that great things may be sought for and received with faith as tiny as a grain of mustard seed. It is not the size of faith that matters, nor the straining of the will to imagine that it will definitely happen, but the genuineness of our trust in God to do things if He pleases.

The Prayer of Faith in James

When James says, 'the prayer of faith shall save the sick,' he does not say that the prayer of faith will heal the sick *every* time, because he has just taught that we should always say, 'If the Lord will' *(James 4.15)*. Nor does he say that the power for healing is in the strength of faith. He simply points out that the anointing with oil (or, literally, the rubbing down with oil) will not heal the sick, but the power of the Lord in answer to prayer. The prayer of faith is not total conviction that the healing will take place (for that is subject to 'if the Lord will'), but sincere belief that God can do anything that He pleases. 'Effectual fervent prayer,' James says, 'availeth much.' However, he also warns that believers may be called to suffer affliction, commending the patience of Job.

The *prayer of faith* is not will-power or forced belief in a definite result, nor is it immense faith, but it is made up of the following components of belief:–

(1) That God has the power to do whatever is asked.

(2) That the Lord is willing to be prevailed upon or 'persuaded' by His people (subject to His supreme wisdom).

(3) That God will hear and answer, although not necessarily in accordance with the solution or time-scale that we have in mind, but according to His wonderful, perfect, kind, wise and sovereign will. When we fail to trust and rest in His supreme judgement, we no longer pray the *prayer of faith*, but a prayer of wilful self-determination.

13

Key Aspects of Prayer

Do You Have a Ministry of Intercession?

I exhort therefore, that, first of all, supplications, prayers, intercessions, and giving of thanks, be made for all men (1 Timothy 2.1).

Praying always with all prayer and supplication in the Spirit, and watching thereunto with all perseverance and supplication for all saints (Ephesians 6.18).

IT IS OFTEN SAID that a priest is one who represents God to man, and who also represents man before God. Christian believers are the 'priests' of the church age, carrying out the first function of a priest in their witness to the unsaved, and the second in pleading for lost souls before the Lord. Do we as individual believers exercise a ministry of intercession? The exhortation of *1 Timothy 2.1* speaks of pleading and making representation for all men, and this definitely includes those who are unconverted, because Paul goes on to say that God 'will have all men to be saved, and to come unto the knowledge of the truth' (verse 4). There falls to every Christian a very remarkable responsibility and privilege, because the God Who commands intercession is undoubtedly moved by intercession, and ready to be prevailed upon, in the mystery of His will.

It is very probable that everyone who reads these words was the subject of someone's earnest intercession prior to their conversion. Who prayed for us? We may not know, but in all likelihood someone was pleading for us. Do we now plead for others? It is not difficult to imagine some of the reasons why the ministry of intercession should have been given to us by the Lord.

Six Fruits of Intercession

First, intercession produces largeness of heart in the interceder, so that we care much more for the souls of others. This ministry makes a great difference to the character of those who take it seriously.

Secondly, it fixes firmly in the believer's heart the mission of Christ as the highest priority in life, because that which occupies our prayer time occupies the very soul, and shapes our values.

Thirdly, the ministry of intercession brings us nearer to Christ in likeness and habit, for He, as our great High Priest, is the eternal Interceder. As He prayed for us (John 17), so we pray for others.

Fourthly (building on our first point), an earnest ministry of intercession for a number of souls helps to make believers outgoing and unselfish.

Fifthly, this is a ministry unlike all others, because it is for every sort of Christian in every kind of situation. It is a ministry for the healthy, and also a ministry for the infirm. Intercession from the sick-bed may, for all we know, be more used than the act of preaching to thousands.

Sixthly – and this is of great significance – intercession firmly establishes in our hearts that all the glory in salvation must be the Lord's. As we pray patiently, the lost are delivered, whereas if we witness without intercession, little ever seems to come of it. By this experience the regular interceder is persuaded beyond all doubt that the power and glory is entirely the Lord's.

What is the *scope* of the ministry of intercession? It extends beyond the following themes, but these represent most of our desires:

♦ The conversion of lost individuals
♦ The blessing of Gospel workers
♦ The preservation and protection of the Lord's people ('Pray one for another,' says James)
♦ The growth and peace of Christians
♦ The instrumentality of Christians
♦ The healing of others
♦ The protection of the young from the world

Abraham's Example of Intercession

The first major example of intercessory prayer in the Bible is that of Abraham pleading for the life of Lot and his household (recorded in *Genesis 18*). The passage in which Abraham 'bargains' with God is well-known, and it contains crucial instructions to us about how we should intercede. When the Lord said He would inspect Sodom, Abraham knew at once that it would be destroyed because of its great evil, and immediately he 'stood yet before the Lord'. Abraham's intercession would not be made merely out of a sense of duty, or lightly, but his mind would be totally engaged, and his heart wholly involved. He clearly believed that his pleading might prevail with the Lord, and so must we. Abraham asks for the sparing of Sodom if fifty righteous souls are found there, appealing to the justice of God. Nevertheless, he is sure that 'the Judge of all the earth' will do what is right, and he assents to God's sovereign and perfect will. We also plead to prevail, but not to dictate to the Lord.

Abraham's language is especially significant when he says, 'Behold now, I have taken upon me to speak unto the Lord, which am but dust and ashes.' He also says a little later, 'Oh let not the Lord be angry, and I will speak yet but this once.' The great patriarch knew that only *humble* intercession is acceptable with God, and we also must grasp this to plead successfully. Abraham's method of humbling himself is to classify himself as mere dust and ashes, and we also should find ways of preparing our hearts in humility. We too may reflect on our unworthiness, foolish deeds, sins of omission and commission, straining of the Lord's patience, and other aspects of our inadequacy before God. We do this to gain a sense of perspective as we plead with the Lord, truly esteeming Him and submitting to Him. The poet James Montgomery captured this approach in his lines –

> *Lord, teach us how to pray aright,*
> *With reverence and with fear;*
> *Though dust and ashes in Thy sight,*
> *We may, we must draw near.*

We note that Abraham's pleadings were heard and answered, but not in the way he expected. The city was destroyed and Lot was saved out of it, a far better solution than that sought by Abraham. The essence of his prayer was rewarded, though not the detail. So it is with us today, as the Lord frequently answers in an ultimately far better way than that requested in our prayers.

The Pleading of Moses for Others

Moses was also a remarkable interceder, pleading repeatedly for the people even when they were murderously hostile toward him.

When God proposed the destruction of the people *(Exodus 32.9ff)*, Moses cried out most passionately for the preservation of the good name and glory of the Lord in the eyes of the Egyptians, pleading the promises that God had made to the patriarchs. The verses recording his prayer must be read by interceders *(Exodus 32.11-13)*, for the Lord accepted that prayer, and Israel was preserved. We learn that intercession must be feelingful and that it is to be carried on regardless of antagonism from those prayed for, its aim being the honour and glory of God.

In the same chapter of *Exodus* we see Moses so filled with desire for the people that he asks to be blotted out of the book of God if it would avail for their deliverance. Astonishingly, this plea follows their wickedness in making the golden calf. The offer was not acceptable with God but the strong feeling behind it, even though the people had made themselves odious to him, indicates how conscientiously he took his responsibility as an intercessor. If only we could accept the same level of responsibility for those among whom the Lord has placed us, our experience of God's blessing of souls would be far greater.

Samuel's Unwavering Intercession

In some ways the most notable intercessor of all was Samuel, the prophet born through prayer, whose name means – 'Asked for of God'. In *1 Samuel 12.23*, he addresses the people saying, 'God forbid that I should sin against the Lord in ceasing to pray for you.' If we neglect to intercede, we sin because we repudiate our priesthood and show great hardness and indifference to others.

We note that Samuel would not *cease* to pray, showing that it was his regular habit to intercede, and for us also there should be daily intercession especially for the conversion of members of our family, selected work colleagues, and other selected unsaved people, especially youngsters connected with our church. If the list of people grows too long, we may need to apportion it across the week, because we should never fall to merely naming names.

The people knew well that Samuel interceded for them, and when under fear or conviction they pressed him to do so *(1 Samuel 12.19)*. Samuel 'cried unto the Lord' for those Israelites, the word 'cried' conveying strong earnestness and desire. Not surprisingly Samuel is specially celebrated in the inspired Word as an intercessor, for in *Psalm 99* we read of 'Moses and Aaron among his priests, and Samuel among them that call upon his name; they called upon the Lord, and he answered them.' In another connection, when the Lord rejects the Jews through the lips of Jeremiah, He discloses: 'Though Moses and Samuel stood before me, yet my mind could not be toward this people' – the astounding implication being the effectiveness of their intercession.

Advice for Interceders

We should pray for more than names, asking *for specific blessings* just as the biblical examples of intercession did, because vague intercession cannot reflect deep concern and desire. We should take each name separately and ask for a distinctive benefit. We should *feel* for those for whom we pray, contemplating, for example, their terrors if lost, or their pain if sick. We should *labour* to represent them, as if we truly desired to persuade the Lord. Earnestness drains very quickly from private prayer if we allow it to do so.

We should pray *persistently* and *regularly* for the lost, never relaxing until the Lord answers from on high (or until the sin unto death is manifested). We should also be careful to respect believers when we pray for them, so that our intercession does not become a superior or condescending act, somehow boosting us, as though we were praying for needy inferiors. The fallen heart is so subtle, and prayer should never be contaminated by a patronising spirit.

We should pray much for our Sunday School class, or whoever else we have special responsibility for. The praying teacher becomes inevitably a visiting teacher, because he or she cares.

We should also give time in intercession for *Christian workers*, both ministers and lay teachers. We should be aware of the *trials* of workers and their *special opportunities*, bringing all as specific matters before the Lord, and we should not forget to rejoice over resulting blessing, and to give thanks.

Once again, the need to pray with *fervour* and *desire* must be emphasised. We need a sense of audience, an atmosphere of awe, and an attitude of humility. If all the members of a church were to engage in personal and consistent intercessory prayer, the outcome would be blessing on a remarkable scale. It is well-known that awakenings have begun with widespread engagement in intercession for people in general and for individuals. If your intercessions are few and small, or repetitive and dispirited, take more seriously this vital and privileged ministry at once. Make a list, and come before the Lord, remembering that in only ten minutes you can intercede for many, but it must be kept up every day. However you pray, remember also that specific prayers, accompanied with a measure of detail, real desire and fervour, are essential in the Christian's 'priestly' intercessory work.

14

Key Aspects of Prayer

Long-Term Praying

Men ought always to pray, and not to faint (Luke 18.1).
Continue in prayer (Colossians 4.2).
Pray without ceasing (1 Thessalonians 5.17).

I F WE NEED the help of God in some situation, or if we are concerned to pray for some person, why must we continue to pray repeatedly and often over a long period? Frequently, it is true, the Lord hears and answers relatively instantly, especially in times of emergency, but equally every praying Christian experiences long waits in prayer, extending even to many years. Sometimes the question is asked whether it is appropriate to pray for the person or situation repeatedly, but it must be because *Colossians 4.2* – 'continue in prayer' – says so. But why? What is God's purpose in this? We would not treat one another in this way, waiting until people had asked us for something fifty times before responding. A number of answers are suggested in the following pages.

Five Reasons for God's Delay

1 God possibly keeps us asking in order to keep our perspectives rightly tuned. He will not allow us to turn Him into a mere servant, constantly at our beck and call. If He did, we would soon be demanding, not asking, 'Do this! Do that!' If He answered all our prayers instantly, our tendency would be to see ourselves as master, and the Lord as a servant existing for our convenience. We would forget to honour Him as supreme and sovereign God. He therefore keeps us waiting and persevering in humble prayer, so that we remember Who He is, and who we are – unworthy creatures saved by grace alone. It is because of our fallen hearts that prayer must be persistent.

2 Then again, God may delay His answers to our prayers to keep reality firmly in our minds. When we are obliged to ask for things repeatedly, it impresses upon our minds the fact that the desired outcome is not a simple matter, and that no human agency could bring it about. Our protracted asking will highlight the greatness of the answer, when it comes. If we prayed once for a sinner to be saved, and the next day he was saved, we would probably cease to believe in the doctrine of total depravity, and reject the idea that the human heart is rebellious, determined and obdurate in its resistance to God. We would believe instead that human beings are really very reasonable, persuadable, open and ready to respond to the Gospel. So the Lord holds us in sound doctrine by keeping us waiting, thereby confirming the teaching of the Word and providing a deep understanding of the difficulty, humanly, of the thing asked for.

3 Similarly, the Lord doubtless delays His response to our prayers to remind us of our own weakness and dependence upon Him. If we had to ask for things only once, we would certainly lose sight

of the extent of our impotence. If we had a thousand great answers to prayer in a single year, so that life was altogether victorious, we would probably swell with spiritual pride imagining that *we* were accomplishing these wonderful things with just a little help from the Lord. However, as the Lord keeps us waiting, we realise that we could *never* bring about the things for which we pray.

Often whole churches experience this delay. They toil long and hard in the visitation of the community and no one responds, and then, once everyone has become convinced that people cannot be persuaded to hear the Word, the Lord moves.

4 It is probable that God has yet another objective in requiring us to persevere in repeated prayer, namely, to remind us of the conditions for prayer. When we have been asking for something for a while, with mounting desire and concern, we begin to wonder, 'Is God withholding His hand because I am not striving to live a holy life, or because I am not witnessing for Him, or reading His Word, or because I am not forgiving someone who has offended against me, or because I am not conducting myself in a true and in a faithful way?' We begin to be challenged, and consider carefully the conditions for prayer. It is by delaying and requiring us to ask repeatedly, that the Lord brings us to this deeper self-examination.

5 Another purpose served by delay in answering prayer is that we soon begin to consider what really matters, and what does not matter. If God answered every request instantly, our prayer agenda might soon resemble a shopping list, greatly extended by requests for unnecessary comforts and luxuries. But when we are required to persevere over months, we usually see that these are unworthy or inappropriate and find it impossible to ask for them repeatedly. We realise that they should be left out of our prayers, and so, delay helps to filter out selfish and worldly petitions. 'O the depth of the riches both of the wisdom and knowledge of God!'

Vigilance in Prayer

Alongside the exhortation to 'continue in prayer,' the apostle says, 'and watch in the same with thanksgiving.' This does not primarily mean that we should watch for the answers, although this is included. It means – keep alert; watch out; keep awake. Our trouble is that in prayer we very soon relax, or lose fervour, going into a kind of automatic mode in which we are not really thinking or longing. To watch, or to keep alert, means firstly that we keep a close watch on the quality, kind and range of our prayers. Are all the forms of prayer represented in our petitions? Are we praying only for ourselves and our own problems? Are we including all aspects of prayer, for example, praise and thoughtful thanksgiving? As we pray for our church and for its witness, do we also pray for power and strength to overcome our sins? There are many matters to pray for, and sometimes we fall into a rut, or into one little compartment of prayer, while the Lord wants us to pray about a whole range of matters.

To watch means also that the answer may bring some new responsibility, to which we must respond. God often answers our prayers by giving us the opportunity to play some part in the outcome. When, for example, we pray for the conversion of someone, the Lord may give us an unparalleled opportunity to speak to that person, but if we are not watching, we may not realise what is happening and be spiritually comatose. We must never pray as though God will look after the entire matter without any action or involvement on our part. God's purpose may be to make us instrumental. We cannot very well pray, 'Lord, save all my colleagues, but please use other instruments, and don't use me because I am embarrassed to witness.'

To *watch* is also to be diligent and methodical. Most people are extremely methodical in managing their secular affairs, poring over bank statements, bills and accounts, and yet, with prayer there is no 'administration' whatsoever – no piece of paper in sight. Prayer should surely be planned in some measure, and reviewed from time to time, and all this is included in the term 'watch'. Never should this greatest of all privileges, the ministry of prayer, be vague, ill-considered, casual or haphazard.

15

Key Aspects of Prayer

Remedies for Problems in Prayer

And Jacob was left alone; and there wrestled a man with him until the breaking of the day. And when he saw that he prevailed not against him, he touched the hollow of his thigh; and the hollow of Jacob's thigh was out of joint, as he wrestled with him (Genesis 32.24-25).

VARIOUS TROUBLES may be experienced from time to time by believers in their life of prayer, and pastors are not excepted. Here are a number of such problems for which solutions will be suggested in this chapter. (We have not included the possibility of hardness of heart resulting from unrepented of serious sin.)

(1) An inability to pray effectually due to lack of assurance.

(2) Coldness of heart, or a lack of desire or enthusiasm (in an otherwise earnest believer).

(3) A strange loss of any sense of a real engagement with God.

(4) Straying thoughts, or short concentration span, or tiredness, often only occurring when in prayer.

(5) Worries crowding in and overpowering prayer.

(6) Forgetfulness of concerns.

(7) A mechanical tendency to pray in the same words for the same things.

(8) The ability to plead fervently undermined by the thought of God's predestination of all things.

(9) The intrusion of anger or resentment over wrongs.

(10) Excessive emotion overtaking prayer and impairing thought.

Praying When Feelings Fail

Let us first take a family of problems, such as lack of assurance, coldness in prayer, little sense of God, and small desire to pray. For a solution we may go to that most famous of texts for troubled minds – *Isaiah 50.10* – 'Who is among you that feareth the Lord, that obeyeth the voice of his servant, that walketh in darkness, and *[yet]* hath no light? let him trust in the name of the Lord, and stay upon his God.'

These words warn that there will be times when feelings, including any clear sense of assurance, will desert a believer, but the instruction of the Lord is that this does not prevent faith and prayer, and therefore we should keep up our spiritual duties, trusting in the name of the Lord and leaning upon our God. In effect, the verse says – 'Your emotional system is no longer co-operating, so that you cannot feel as you would like to do. The enemy of your soul is probably taking advantage of this and is attacking you, but this does not disqualify your prayer.' In these circumstances, as we have advised earlier in these pages, you should come before the Lord without the help or co-operation of feelings, and use your mind alone, falling back on faith only. If you cannot pray with your head and heart together, you must pray with your head only. When emotions are unresponsive, you may feel you have changed, but God has not changed, and the same gracious God Who hears and answers the prayers of His people will hear you. You must trust Him. That is the counsel of *Isaiah 50.10.*

Once we accept that legitimate prayer may be made with only the mind functioning we will find it easier to pray. Once we realise that prayer does not depend upon a sense of assurance, nor even a sensed engagement with God, we are able to get down to the task. It may even be that this is the kind of prayer with which God is most pleased. We remember Satan's claim that Job did not serve God for nothing, and if his blessings were removed his insincerity would be exposed. The Lord allowed Job's blessings to be withdrawn, but Job never abandoned his belief in the Lord. Certainly, he voiced many unworthy complaints, and behaved insolently toward God, but always his preoccupying concern was to find why God dealt with him as He did, and never to deny Him. Satan was proved wrong.

Satan is convinced that we too serve God only while good feelings are present. The Lord, in a sense, replies in *Isaiah 50.10* saying, 'My servant will seek Me even if his mind is all that is left to him. He will take full advantage of it and will pray with that alone.' Satan will be proved wrong in our case also if we keep up prayer regardless of how we feel. God looks upon us with special pleasure when we press on and pray without the help of sensed assurance and warm feelings, for this is 'raw' faith, unassisted and unadorned by secondary comforts. Therefore we should summon all our mental powers to engage in a full programme of praise and prayer, theoretical as it may feel, trusting that God will in due time restore the heart to feel.

We are also helped to pray by the realisation that failure to pray steals praise from God, depriving Him of His due. We may not feel as we would like to, but we still owe Him a debt of thanksgiving and worship and must not deny Him that. Even if praise is rendered with the mind only, it is entirely valid and acceptable before God, because the mind is the most important department of the soul, and the palace of faith.

Prayer Troubles in the Psalms

When we pray with the mind alone, the heart often responds, as we see in the examples of prayer in the *Psalms*. Some haunting words of David in *Psalm 13* show his sad heart melting following an emphatic affirmation of God's faithfulness, with the result that the shadows lifted, and assurance returned. Isaac Watts puts the sense of David's words into a magnificent hymn of experience:

> *How long wilt Thou conceal Thy face?*
> *My God, how long delay?*
> *When shall I feel those heavenly rays*
> *That chase my fears away?*
>
> *See how the prince of darkness tries*
> *All his malicious arts:*
> *He spreads a mist around my eyes,*
> *And throws his fiery darts.*
>
> *How would the tempter boast aloud*
> *If I became his prey!*
> *And how the sons of earth grow proud*
> *At Thy so long delay.*
>
> *But hell shall fly at Thy rebuke,*
> *And Satan hide his head;*
> *He knows the terrors of Thy look,*
> *And hears Thy voice with dread.*
>
> *Thou wilt display that sovereign grace*
> *Where all my hopes have hung:*
> *I shall employ my heart in praise,*
> *And victory shall be sung.*

By the end of the psalm, praise is again on David's lips, and we should learn that to recount God's goodness, and to affirm His mercies, even when we *feel* little, often leads to a good measure of returning joy.

In *Psalm 56* David follows the same procedure, expressing his trust in God in the darkest circumstances, reflecting on the goodness of the Lord and His Word, and subsequently finding his feelings joining with his mind. The psalmist's words in *Psalm 61* ring true for all believers at some time – 'When my heart is overwhelmed: lead me to the rock that is higher than I.' Once again, reflection, affirmation and thanksgiving soon lift the psalmist in heart.

Psalm 42 – unascribed – is a great example of how a clear affirmation in prayer of our belief in God's faithfulness can lift our spirits, and Asaph's *Psalm 77* also demonstrates the value of praise to rekindle dormant feelings. We should review and rehearse in praise all our blessings, as well as God's supreme goodness, and never lapse into forlorn prayerlessness.

To the exercise of praise we add two further measures for coldness of heart, the first being the practice of reviewing in detail the many significant answers to prayer which the Lord has given in past weeks – even months and years. We should press the mind to go back and acknowledge the ways of God, and thank Him. It may be helpful to put a list of significant answers in writing, so that these can be called to mind readily in prayer.

Earlier in this book we mentioned one remedy for 'feelings' problems, which is to put intercession first in our prayers. If we are cold and spiritually detached when we go to pray, to plead for others makes us less concerned about our own feelings and trials, and more focused on their spiritual needs, and this often helps us to regain fervour of heart. Our ministry of intercession is not only a means of blessing to others, but a means of blessing to us also.

Remedies for Mental Tiredness

What can be done when tiredness, short concentration span, or forgetfulness strike the time of prayer? The most obvious remedy is to pray more briefly, more often. We should pray several times in the day as opportunity arises, and make greater use of 'emergency' prayers of a few sentences, as occasion requires. Multiple prayer is mentioned by David in *Psalm 55* (one of his psalms of distress) – 'Evening, and morning, and at noon, will I pray' (v 17). Frequency in prayer definitely helps one over the tiredness problem.

Roaming thoughts and lack of concentration can also be countered by breaking up a prayer time into portions. When thoughts begin to wander, stop the prayer and wait or read for five minutes before resuming. Another well-tried help for sustaining concentration is to use notes in prayer, a method all should try at some time if only to train oneself to be thorough. In times when thoughts are distracted it is especially valuable. Write down your agenda for prayer, rejecting any idea that this remedy is trivial. List all the situations and people for whom you should pray, including detail, then refer to the list through the time of prayer. Let the list provide the structure, and prayer will be clothed with serious purpose. It is good to note down different details for each topic day by day, so that consecutive prayer sessions are never exactly the same. This helps to maintain concentration and a serious sense of purpose.

The next piece of advice might seem to be in breach of the 'vain repetition' rule, but this is not really the case. If the mind is tired and slow to summon a pleading spirit and to wing a thought heavenward, it can be helpful to pray for everything twice. A restatement of each thought to help one to focus often kindles earnestness. It is not perhaps a good habit *always* to pray in this way, but it will frequently make prayer more meaningful. It does not transgress the Saviour's stricture against vain repetition because the purpose is to establish sincerity and full mental assent to the petition, not to encourage empty and futile incantations or mutterings.

Praying With Scripture

Another precious and well-tried word of advice which greatly assists tired minds is to pray *with* the Scripture. For your devotional time select a passage of Scripture (*Ephesians* would be an example of one that really lends itself to this), and read a verse or a line, and then pray it. Thank God for this truth, whatever it may be. Praise Him for it. Worship Him for that promise, or duty or exhortation, and for what it means. Submit to it and pledge obedience. Repent if convicted by any word. Then read the next verse or line and pause again to reflect and pray. In doing this we let the Word of God determine what we pray for, and shut ourselves in with the Lord's own words. This will obviously not complete all our responsibilities in prayer, but it may prove immensely helpful in times of special need for bringing the heart to life.

Dealing With Unwanted Thoughts

What remedy is there for anger, inner bitterness, jealousy, or any other unwanted thoughts or feelings which may invade the time of prayer? These must always be very decisively and firmly rejected and expelled from the mind. Mortify, that is put to death, the evil or inappropriate thoughts. It may be that these thoughts invade the prayer time because they have been allowed to roam freely in our minds for some time. In other words we have not resolved them by prayer and submission to God's providence, but have inflamed them with self-pity, or with resentment toward whoever has wronged us. If so, there are attitudes to be repented of before going to prayer. But if the unwanted thoughts or feelings are justifiable grief or disappointment, we should still set a limit on the amount of time we allow to these thoughts, firmly placing a barrier on them for the time of prayer. Some of the remedies already mentioned for coldness or poor attention-span will help to hold the mind on to the prayer-agenda, alongside the making of a solemn pledge to give no room to the unwanted thoughts.

The Problem of Foreordination

Fatalism will inevitably empty prayer of fervour. It is hard to pray for the sick if we add to every plea '*if it be Thy will*' in a resigned tone. To use these words is right, but to understand them in a fatalistic way is wrong. We must remind ourselves that God employs prayer as *part* of His process of blessing, making it instrumental. He commands us to pray with fervency for a purpose, and not because He intends to ignore us altogether.

If the writer may be permitted another personal recollection – this was a hindrance for me in spiritual youth, when first grasping the doctrines of sovereign grace. The usual way of describing how God is the author of all effective prayer is to say that He ordains not only the *ends* (the answer) but also the *means* (the prayer itself), and in a sense this is true. I was taught that every inclination to pray is from God (which is correct), but it was explained in a very mechanistic way, undermining personal responsibility. If I did not pray, it could well have been God's fault, not mine, for not having impelled me to pray in a sufficiently irresistible way.

However, the teaching just described runs the risk of forgetting the mysterious interface between God's foreordination and the believer's obedience. God's foreordination of my prayers as a converted person is not quite the same as His foreordination of my salvation. In the latter case He brings it about by irresistible grace. It may have seemed to me that I chose Him gladly, willingly and freely, but the reality is that He changed my heart, making me willing to listen, bending my stubborn will, bringing light into my darkened mind, and placing my conscience under conviction of sin. The moment I became a believer, however, a new margin of responsibility came into my relationship with God, and into my responses to His promptings.

In the Scripture, God calls me to prayer, and I must respond. He promises blessing if I do so. Certainly, He stirs my heart and gives the desire – but I may still fail to pray. Is it God's fault? Has He left out some vital 'link' in His prompting of me? No, it is my fault, and in not praying I shall forfeit blessing.

We may, according to God's Word, truly prevail upon Him. He evidently took account of our prayers before the foundation of the world. He is pleased to hear us pray, and undertakes to respond. It is ever true – 'Ye have not because ye ask not.'

Let us never slip into fatalism by a misunderstanding of God's foreordination. Fervour will be kindled when we have a solid hope that God will take account of our cries, and is persuadable by His people, according to His own secret and mysterious will. We must take at face value the words of Christ, and also those given to John:–

'Ask, and it shall be given you; seek, and ye shall find; knock, and it shall be opened unto you' *(Matthew 7.7)*.

'And this is the confidence that we have in him, that, if we ask any thing according to his will, he heareth us' *(1 John 5.14)*.

Why Do We Need to Ask in Prayer?

Problems in prayer are often eased when we reflect on the purposes that lie behind asking prayer. (The purposes in this summary have mostly been referred to in the course of this book.)

1 We are called to ask in prayer because prayer establishes God's *sovereignty*, might and majesty. The simple fact that we have to

ask God for all our blessings, and then give thanks for them, reinforces in our minds that God is our governor and provider, and that we need His guidance, permission and provision in everything. If we did not have to pray, this vital awareness would surely drop out of our minds, and so prayer keeps us under God's authority.

2 Prayer also makes us deeply aware of God's goodness. Whenever we repent, we taste His forgiving love, and when we cry out for deliverance or light in some trial, He intervenes and helps us, leaving us in wonder at His kindness. If such blessings were given without our engaging in prayer, we would not truly appreciate His goodness and power.

3 Prayer also brings believers into fellowship or interaction with God. Would we fellowship much in conversation with the Lord if we did not need to ask for our blessings?

4 Prayer teaches us about our privileged position as believers. What greater privilege can there be than to have access to a mighty God Who is willing to be prevailed upon by His people! We may have no power of audience with the great ones of this world, and even if we had, there is little likelihood that we could influence them. Yet we may go to the King of kings and Lord of lords, and be efficaciously heard.

5 Prayer, like nothing else, and in the kindest way, teaches us our limitations and inadequacy. In the Garden of Eden, Adam and Eve wanted independence, believing that God was withholding from them powers and insight which would enable them to succeed without Him. Through prayer God trains us to go in the opposite direction, and to see our need of Him in everything.

6 Prayer also helps to deliver us from pride. If churches filled up without prayer, preachers would think of themselves very highly and take all the credit. If we could live holy lives, or accomplish

anything of substance without prayer, conceit would drown us. Prayer maintains our perspective and keeps us humble.

7 Prayer also delivers from self-interest and selfishness, because it helps us to realise we cannot have and do whatever we like. Earthly aims and selfish things 'stick in the gullet' of a praying believer. The need to ask the Lord about every major thing we do or buy serves as a restraint upon our appetites. Without prayer we might easily make carnal decisions, but we dare not ask God's blessing upon excessive and self-vaunting things. Prayer therefore serves as a caution, and helps us to be better people. We know we must pray for others, and as we do so we become much more concerned about them than about ourselves. Therefore, by prayer, we are to a large extent delivered from the idol 'self'.

8 Prayer always builds up faith, as one's memory bank of God's answers grows. At times the Lord delays His response until we pray repeatedly and more earnestly, all this being a trust-strengthening process. The powerful evidence of answers in the past develops in us a tenacious trust that He will bless in His perfect way, in due time.

9 Alongside faith prayer produces assurance. Many times when feelings fail, the evidence of God's fatherly goodness is derived from answered prayer. Nothing is so melting as great answers to prayer.

10 Prayer, to a remarkable extent, makes the believer aware that he is never alone. We can pray whatever our circumstances, and wherever we are.

11 Prayer also is a great leveller, teaching us that not one of God's servants is greater in His sight than any other. Paul pleads for prayer as though his usefulness depended upon it – and it did. The people had a share in his ministry by prayer, remembering

that as a needy mortal, he was like them. Knowing how much he depended on the prayers of others, Paul also was delivered from exalted views of himself.

12 Prayer inevitably promotes repentance, because the very act of approaching the Lord makes true believers ashamed of their sin, and moves them to seek cleansing.

WHEN the Saviour taught His disciples this prayer, He had not yet instructed them to always address the Father in His own name. But the time came when this all-important principle for Christians would be clearly expressed. Looking ahead to His resurrection and ascension, and the era that would follow, the Lord announced the golden rule:

'And in that day ye shall ask me nothing. Verily, verily, I say unto you, Whatsoever ye shall ask the Father in my name, he will give it you. Hitherto have ye asked nothing in my name: ask, and ye shall receive, that your joy may be full' *(John 16.23-24)*.

Both audio and video on-line sermons of Dr Masters, preached at the Metropolitan Tabernacle, are available on the Tabernacle's main website: www.MetropolitanTabernacle.org

Audio messages of Sunday and mid-week ministry may be either downloaded or streamed, and video messages are also available for streaming.

An audio-video cassette and CD catalogue may be obtained from: Metropolitan Tabernacle, Elephant & Castle, London SE1 6SD email: cassettes@MetropolitanTabernacle.org